IN THE BLINK OF AN EYE

A SCHOOL SHOOTING SURVIVOR'S JOURNEY OF
TRAGEDY, TRIBULATION, AND TRIUMPH

Nathaniel R. Tavarez

AMERICAN PRODIGY
Publishing

Published by American Prodigy Publishing

Cover design by 99 Designs
Book Design by Nathaniel Tavarez

ISBN 979-8-9893897-2-8 (eBook)
ISBN 979-8-9893897-1-1 (Paperback)
ISBN 979-8-9893897-0-4 (Hardcover)

Printed in the United States of America

CONTENTS

INTRODUCTION
HOW THIS BOOK CAME TO BE

Now, when it comes to the context throughout this story, I did my absolute best to show you every experience, including the good and the bad and everything in between, so that you can get the greatest picture of my experiences to understand then why I have rooted myself within the nation-wide mission you will get to know more about towards the end of this book.

As the writer, I poured countless emotions into every single word that you see on every page of this book. In fact, it took me approximately three consecutive years to write this book, following the other four years where I debated even starting it, which consisted of countless prayers, hours upon hours of typing, and endless revisions to make it as perfect as possible for a great reader experience, and many tears where I questioned if I was the right person to tell this kind of story while attempting to bring together a community around the mission I have. My goal as you read this is that you're able to gain quality insight as to what was all going through my head during the tragedy, that you can discern all of my experiences while amidst the tribulations, and that you can join in with me while celebrating every single win where we were truly able to find triumph. I pray that every word of this book touches the hearts of all who read it and helps to guide you toward an even better life while calling you to whatever place the Lord has set out for you so that together, we can make the world an even better place.

If you'd like to get an even deeper look into the experiences throughout this story, feel free to visit www.nathanielspeaks.com/behind-the-lid or scan the QR Code below to see various pictures, videos, and other types of media that relate back to each piece of this story in every chapter. Wishing you the best reading experience throughout this entire book and hope that you feel called to create an even better life for yourself and those you love daily. Thank you for your investment, support, and time. I'll see you in Chapter One!

- Nathaniel

www.nathanielspeaks.com/behind-the-lid

Password: BLINK

CHAPTER ONE
A NEW YEAR WITH BIG ASPIRATIONS

*"You have brains in your head. You have feet in your shoes.
You can steer yourself in any direction you choose."
- Dr. Seuss*

My 6:00 a.m. alarm is going off, and after reaching to snooze it three times, it's already 6:32 a.m. At that point, I am barely rolling out of bed with an hour to shower, get ready, and rush out the door to catch the bus. Before I even step out the door, a million thoughts ran through my head because it's a day of many new beginnings for me. It's my first day of 7th grade at a new school, not to mention the first time I am riding the bus to school.

I get to my bus stop, and a younger girl and a boy stand there laughing their heads off. I approach them curiously, with the first words out of my mouth being, "What's so funny?". The girl says, "He just farted," and continues laughing uncontrollably. So I ask them, "Are y'all brother and sister?" assuming they are, being his comfort of blowing fumes out in front of her. Indeed, they were brother and sister, Tyler and Abbie. Little did I know, the two of them would be the ones who helped me initially break my social shell. So the bus pulled up, and we got on and sat pretty close to each other. My goal this year was to make tons of new friends, so I knew I had to start talking with other people immediately to achieve that goal. So I am sitting next to a girl who has her earbuds in. I turn to look out the window beside her, and she turns to me. I frantically turned away when we made initial eye contact, worried she thought I was staring at her. She takes off her earbuds and says, "Hey! What's your name? Are you excited about the first day of school? Because I know I am!" So I tell her my name and mention that I am excited to be starting at a new school and ask for her name. Her name is Kara, and she's now telling me all about the school, including which teachers I should take next year and which bathrooms to avoid. Then, the bus stops, and it is time for all of us to get off and head inside for the first day of school. Thankfully, I knew where my first class was since I had found it during orientation last week.

As I stepped into the classroom, I locked eyes with Aria, a girl I hadn't seen in years. It was so exciting because she was my very first best friend, whom I hadn't seen since preschool, and now we have our first-period class together. I rush up to say hi and sit in the seat next to her. We start talking and catching up on all the things that have happened since we last saw each other, and then, this guy Carson walks up to interrupt our conversation and tells me I am sitting in his spot, hinting that I need to find somewhere else to sit. I laugh and tell him, "I'm good right here, but thanks for the suggestion." It was probably not smart of me to make that first impression on people, being that I was at a new school. Yet, I don't allow many people—if any—to talk down to me like that, so I thought it was pretty funny. Then the bell rang to go to our second-period class. I was nervous about this course in particular. It wasn't because of the whole shy attitude I was feeling but because it was an English class on top of being the first honors class I had ever taken. The anxiety took over, and my shyness snuck back in with no speed limit. After we sat down, our teacher told us to pick a partner, as that's who we would begin our readings with. I sat there nervously, and by the time I looked up, everyone already had a partner, or so I thought. One other guy was sitting in the corner, so the teacher put us together for the collaborative reading session. Little did I know we would partner up on a few other projects together throughout the semester. I can honestly say that most of the time, he taught me a large majority of the content we had to complete on each assignment because of his level of intelligence. This kid is one who you knew was going to an Ivy League college, without a doubt. As the rest of the day passed, the last bell rang to release us from class.

I loaded back up on the bus and sat right next to Kara, the girl I sat with on the way to school this morning. We talked the whole ride back to her stop, and then it was time I got off at the next stop. Remember Tyler and Abbie, the brother and sister I mentioned earlier? Well, they got off right behind me. As the bus drove away, the three of us stood there talking about our first day, and yet again, Tyler was talking out of his butt, literally. I could have sworn some green fumes were lingering behind that kid, and I wasn't about to stand there and smell it, so I quickly made my way back home.

I walked in the door to an empty house since my parents were still at work. It was time that I made myself my regularly scheduled bowl of ramen noodles, the chicken flavor mixed with the beef flavor, to be exact. As I heated them up in the microwave, I turned on the TV to watch my favorite show of all time, Teen Wolf. I planned to watch at least two episodes until my parents got home and started prepping for dinner. I was getting so deep into the show that I didn't think to look down at my phone and see when they were getting home. The tension rose when Scott and Derek started wolfing out on each other again at the Hale house in the middle of the woods. Around this part of the episode, I heard the little beeping sounds at the front door where my mom was putting in the code to unlock the door. She walks in, and my dad follows her not long after. We sat at the bar top and enjoyed a great-tasting pork chop with beans and golden potatoes. I told them stories about how great my day had gone and how I believed I would really like this new school.

Days and weeks went by, and I made a ton of new friends. At that point, I felt accomplished, especially since making new friends was a goal of mine at the start of the school year. Every day at lunch, I would sit with mostly the same group of people. Mind you, that group of people took up an entire lunch table. Every once in a while, I would sit at a few other tables to spend time with all the other friends I had made in my first few weeks there.

As time passed, the new school became a place where I felt like I belonged. One of my friends had actually turned out to be a somewhat distant relative to my sister-in-law, B. We had found this out because my brother and sister-in-law were expecting, and my friend Sammie and I crossed paths during the transition from a baby shower to a pamper party, and that's where we discovered the family relations. After that point, we often talked about it in school as we were both excited. I couldn't stop talking about it because I couldn't wait to be an uncle. After what felt like years—which was really just a few more weeks—B was really close to her due date. One day after school, my sister had picked me up and drove me back to the house. As soon as we drove up, my mom jumped into the car and said that we should head to the hospital as she believed my sister-in-law might be in labor, and they didn't allow her to text us. As we were only a few blocks down from the hospital, my sister-in-law sent a text saying that the baby didn't have a heartbeat and they would have to induce her for a natural birth. As we walked into the hospital, the medical staff had to place me in a room and shut the door as I had completely lost my mind at this point, and I could only imagine the pain my sister-in-law and brother were in. Up to this point in my life, I don't think I have ever experienced such pain having to see them go through this. All I know is my niece was the most beautiful little girl I had ever seen, and I prayed to God over and over again to bring her back. Yet I wasn't sure at that particular moment if He would do it as He may have had different plans. Knowing that we would have to mourn from that point forward, all I could do was pray that the Lord help my brother and sister-in-law to find peace and never have to experience this again. Every Sunday after church, my parents and I would drive over to visit the baby at the cemetery. It was still difficult, yet I had started feeling a sense of peace as I had almost felt her presence with us.

Once life began to shift back to as close as normal as it could get, I continued on with school even though I wasn't in the mood for it or anything else really. In fact, there was an announcement made one morning that there would be basketball tryouts toward the end of the semester, and I questioned if I should try out or not, although I had to convince myself that I was ready for it. Sports were my favorite thing to do as I was growing up, and it was time for me to start my transition from the little league to the middle school level. The day comes for tryouts, and it is also the last day of school before winter break. I enter the locker room, suit up for the court, and head out to stretch before drills. Coach calls us up to the edge of the court and tells us to set up for one-on-one three-point drills. As we begin to partner up for the drill, I have the ball, and one of the well-known athletes around town who's pretty talented was defending. I was a little nervous because I had never been all that great at sports. However, I was determined to prove my potential to make the team. As soon as the coach blew the whistle, I dribbled a few times to free up some space to take a clean shot. As I hopped up for the jump shot, I let out a sigh of relief with a giant smile on my face, as I had just juked out a guy who claimed to be unstoppable on the court. I stood wide-eyed for a minute, as you could hear the swish of the net echo across the gym while everyone was collectively wide-eyed and silent. Then I walked off the court with a smirk on my face because of the trash he was talking to me before the drill. What I didn't realize is that this kid would hate me for embarrassing him on the court from that point forward. I thought it was hilarious because he was a bully, and I don't deal with bullies. He simply hated that I showed him up at that moment when everyone was looking. As we closed out our drills and wrapped up tryouts, it was time to find out which of us would make the team. As expected, the coach called out the names of all the guys who were pretty darn good. Then, we heard the coach call out the names of those whose parents are coaches or teachers or who simply have a lot of money. Funny enough, the coach didn't select me for the team because I didn't fit into any of those categories despite showing up his "top player" during the drills.

As soon as I went home, I got over it because I didn't want to be on the same team as a guy who planned to ruin me—which I wouldn't allow to happen anyway—and waste my time to satisfy other people's evil humor. I liked the fact that I could do better things than sit on the bench, watching people play a sport that I love and knew I was decently good at. Plus, if I am going to watch guys play basketball, I'd rather get into some great NBA Basketball games on ESPN. Plus, I was excited to be on winter break and be free to go places and do things. As my family and I began to prepare for the holiday season, we went on a shopping trip in the northern part of the state to buy all the presents to make this Christmas season extra special, even though spending time with family was the best part, no matter the presents under the tree. Christmas came quicker than we expected. As soon as the day hit, we started cooking up the sumptuous meals we only make on Christmas every year. Then came the time to open our presents. The cool thing is, I was super blessed to get everything I had asked for, and it was perfect. The only thing which slightly sucks is school starts back up in a couple of weeks. I had an awesome break though, and the new year felt like a great place to help me move forward with all the crazy things I was doing at this time.

Then, it came time to head back to school. The date we are supposed to start is January 13th, 2014. I didn't care about that too much anymore because I was excited about the fact that my dad bought me a ticket to attend a baseball clinic that was starting the weekend before I headed back to school. It will be a weekend trip up to the northern part of the state for the following 7 weeks. After loading up the truck to head out of town, we made our usual stop at "the burrito" to get my favorite breakfast burrito filled with egg, potato, chorizo, and cheese with guacamole. The funny thing is, it's always nap time for me after eating those huge burritos, as I can only imagine how many carbs they have. After quite a long nap on the drive upstate, I began to finish suiting up. I slipped on my cleats so I could head straight out to the field as soon as the car stopped, even though I was ready to roll out before Dad hit the brakes since I was so excited about this baseball clinic.

We walked up toward the table to sign in, and from there, the camp staff sent me straight out to the field for warm-ups. The trainers paired me with a guy who had a wicked throw. Whenever he threw the baseball to me, my hand would feel a shocking, needle-like sensation. I began laughing and then threw it back harder since he seemed like a guy who was a little too confident in himself. We finished up with warm-ups and transitioned to our pitching training on the mound. I loved being the pitcher, so this was exciting for me. I learned more about pitching in that short time we spent on the mound than I did playing the last five or six years in the little league. Batting training was up next, and that was the last training session of the day. After the coaches taught me a technique they teach their high school and college players, I was hitting so well.

I knew when I stepped up to the plate at my next baseball game, I'd be hitting the ball over the fence, or at least dang close to it.

The time at the clinic went by so quickly it was already time to head back home. As we pulled into the driveway, I shoved all my stuff into my bag while thinking about which Christmas presents I would take with me to school and tell my friends about. Then, as I got inside and my head hit the pillow, I was out. The alarm clock went off shortly after, and I was happy I had a full day to relax and watch some more Teen Wolf before returning to school. As bedtime was getting closer, I decided to lay out some of the cool clothes I had just got for Christmas and chose which things I would wear to school that next day. A great night's sleep followed quickly after. As soon as I woke up, I jumped in the shower to start getting ready. When I hopped out of the shower, I noticed the news channel was on in the living room. At the bottom of the screen, the meteorologist displayed many school delays and cancellations resulting from the weekend snowstorm. It just happened to be that my school was the one that came across the screen. Immediately after, the school notified my mom of the school cancellation that day because of a main water break. I decided to take another day to relax and have some time to myself. After my parents got home, we ate dinner and went straight to bed. I knew I was fixing to have an interesting night of sleep before school started back again because now my excitement was extremely high, with all kinds of thoughts running through my head about how I wanted to make every day count before the end of the school year. It turns out that it was such an interesting night of sleep I woke up feeling sick and nearly considered staying home. Fighting through the nausea, I powered through it and took my morning shower. Thankfully, I felt pretty well after my shower, so I finished getting ready, said bye to momma, and headed to the bus stop.

As usual, I see the siblings hanging out at the bus stop. While walking up, Tyler lets out another cheek flapper while Abbie asks me what I got for Christmas. We talked for a few minutes, and then the bus came screeching around the corner. We loaded in and were officially off to our first day back to school. I sat right next to Kara, as I now have a habit of doing, and we were catching up since we hadn't been on the bus with each other for a while now. The bus got to school a lot quicker than usual—or so it seemed—but we were happy that we had listened to all of our favorite songs on the playlist before getting off the bus. Usually, we would offload the bus and head straight to the football field before we went inside for our first-period class. The ground was still a little icy, and the temperature outside felt exactly that of freezing cold. The school staff began directing us to the school's front entrance so we could go into the big gym and stay warm before class. As soon as I walked into the gym, I saw my friends toward the bottom row of the bleachers. I walked straight up to them and sat down to start talking all about the cool adventures we had during the break. I rotated my body around a little so we could have this little circle for good conversation since I was sitting at the very bottom and some of my friends were behind me. Little did I know, in the blink of an eye, that my life would soon be changed forever!

CHAPTER TWO
TRAGEDY STRIKES

"Tough times never last,
but tough people do."
– Robert H. Schuller

The world felt at a complete standstill as my body fell straight to the ground, and I was completely blinded. My adrenaline kicked in so fast that I couldn't perceive the passage of time. All I could hear was a deafening sound in my ears, and classmates were screaming all around me. I immediately tried to stand, clutching my face, believing the school had exploded and felt like my body blew straight into the air, past the bus stop that I got dropped off at ten minutes earlier. A teacher approached me and gently guided me to relax on the floor, saying that everything would be alright and that my mom wasn't here but that she would be my momma for now. She said I would be famous someday, my face would be on billboards, and they would make a movie about me. As she continued communicating with me, I lightly drifted to a calm state. I suddenly felt something—likely a textbook in my backpack—poking my back, so the only words that came out of my mouth were, "Take off my backpack." Then, my vision went completely black, and I was unconscious, giving complete control to God. Little did I know, a school shooter fired a gun ten feet in front of me, and hundreds of lead pellets infiltrated my body. When I thought I had peacefully passed out, my heart had stopped entirely, with no pulse to be found. I wasn't breathing for the next eight minutes. I was assumed to be dead until the paramedics could finally enter the building, as this was the same exact time I began to gasp for air. Throughout the initial timeframe, while I was on the floor, my classmates were thankfully able to make it safely into a classroom and remain on lockdown until the scene was declared safe by law enforcement.

A police officer dropped his son off at the front immediately after the shooter discharged the weapon. After being notified by the principal that someone had just fired a gun in the big gym, the officer darted into the school, assessing every area to detect the active threat. As he made it to the big gym and approached the shooter, Officer Parker asked him to get on the ground with his hands behind his back. The shooter proceeded to calmly turn around with his hands behind him as instructed, and Officer Parker pushed forward to lay him on the ground, placing the handcuffs on his wrists. Once officers detained the shooter and escorted him out of the gym, the paramedics safely rushed inside, rapidly assessed my injuries, tore off all my clothes, and loaded me into the ambulance.

They drove me over to our local hospital as quickly as possible. After seeing that my injuries were of such significant complexity that they couldn't help me, the nurses bandaged up a large portion of my body from the top of my head all the way down to my waist to slow the bleeding and transport me to a hospital with all the necessary equipment and surgeons. As they were wheeling me back out of the hospital to load me into the MedEvac, my mom had just arrived, and they zoomed my stretcher past her as she told me, "You are going to be fine, baby. God bless you. I love you mijo."

The helicopter was lifted urgently into the air as they flew me to the Level I Trauma Center in Lubbock. There was so much going on after we ascended, being that I was still bleeding from multiple areas of my body. At one point, the paramedics had to insert an IV into my hand to push a medication called epinephrine that would help to keep my heart beating. Under the intense pressure, considering the situation, the IV infiltrated, causing my vein to explode, and the medication flooded into the various layers of tissue in my hand, which created a humongous blister. Once we landed on the helicopter pad, the flight staff rolled me out to transfer care to the trauma center. The healthcare professionals proceeded to wheel me into the hospital to get me inside the operating room. Being my age, they needed parental consent for much of what they had to do to save my life. Luckily, my dad was already in Lubbock for a work trip and at the hospital before we landed. The doctors handed him a stack of papers to sign, and all he could say was to do whatever they needed to do to keep me alive. I entered the operating room around eleven o'clock that morning, and the surgeons operated on me until about midnight that night, totaling approximately 13 hours on the table. The main priority at the time was to take out a large portion of my skull in order to let my brain relax because of the significant swelling from the pellet that entered and was now at the very center. The general surgeon made an incision from my lower chest down to my waist—often referred to as an exploratory surgery—where they determined which of my organs were damaged and stopped the internal bleeding. It happens to be that some of the pellets nicked my heart. Amidst the chaos, the eye surgeon had to do his best to examine my eyes and see what he could do to save them. My left eye had been split in half, which he stitched back together as opposed to taking it out entirely for the sake that I am a child, and my right eye experienced a 90% retinal detachment. Thankfully, "righty" had the potential to regain vision in the distant future. Yet, there was no hope for "lefty" aside from the eye doctor giving him a chance with the hope of future medical advancements. During that time, my body experienced a few other operations. I underwent approximately ten operations, with several more to come. Following hours upon hours in surgery, my body was finally stable enough to be transported into the Pediatric

Intensive Care Unit (PICU).

The nurse practitioner wheeled me into room 256 and brought my family in shortly after to see me. My entire body swelled, and my skin turned purple, resembling a giant bruise covering every inch of my physical being. Hundreds of tiny blood spots covered my face and chest, visible where bandages, my gown, or my neck brace didn't cover. The left side of my head became disfigured, as it was the area where my skull had been removed, along with my swollen brain throbbing out. Then I had tubes in my head, nose, chest, and mouth that were either draining fluids, breathing for me, or feeding me. It would be at least a week before I would be able to be taken out of the medical sedation to allow my body plenty of time to heal. However, that expected duration was under the best-case scenario. The doctors relentlessly questioned my ability to talk, eat, and move again, mainly because of the single pellet that had penetrated directly to the center of my brain, as I mentioned earlier, which would cause more harm or possible death if they attempted to remove it. If anything was going through my head at that time, it was the thought of knowing the road to recovery would be long, yet I know that with God, all things are possible.

CHAPTER THREE
THE ROAD TO RECOVERY

*"It always seems
impossible until it's done."*
– Nelson Mandela

In the world inside my mind, I was already feeling free. Free of worry, fear, and pain. Dreams were very much present, imaginatively representing a universe of my own wild creation. It was pitch dark outside, and I suited up in what seemed to be military gear. I jumped into a tanker with fellow soldiers and maneuvered to the squadron to board the helicopter. Once we loaded in, we flew over a beautiful stadium that was lighting up the sky. Right beside it was the biggest billboard that I had ever seen. I was in complete awe while trying to process what was on it. The picture showed a great shot of me, featured as the next player's face on the NBA2K video game case. Following a rapid descent towards the landing zone, the arena personnel guided me into the stadium, which was entirely empty. I was sitting on a giant chair in the center of a never-ending room lit dimly with the most elegant light fixtures. A professional jeweler was fitting my finger for a pure gold championship ring. It was like I was on top of the world.

The dream scene quickly shifted into a different story. Oddly enough, I was walking through a cemetery, which was frightening at first. In fact, it was the cemetery in my hometown. I walked up to one of the grave sites, which happened to be the place where my beautiful niece had been buried a few months before the shooting. The craziest part was that she had no longer been buried in the ground and had already grown to appear like a toddler, dancing around like the happiest baby in the world, clothed in her white dress. I think my heart was smiling, literally.

A rapid shift to the dream scene came, and I was lying in a hospital bed this time. While looking to my left, I saw a man's face who I felt like I'd known forever. He was my nurse who I would always be shouting out to by screaming, "GREYSON" to get his attention. I wanted him to take me outside to get some fresh air. He placed me in a wheelchair and took me outside. I was relieved as soon as the doors opened. I could finally breathe the purest of air and see how beautiful the nature surrounding me was—especially the sunrise view, as that has always been a favorite of mine. The scenes of the world inside my head continued to change, and everything was so good, with everlasting joy in my own little world. Yet, it finally came time to determine if I would be able to come out of the medically induced coma and wake up in the real world.

Doctors were still questioning if I was going to be able

to wake up and, if so, working to analyze if I would be able to eat, speak, move, or do any other things on my own that the average twelve-year-old boy should be able to do. I woke up and couldn't see anything. My vision appeared absent, as if the world was now in complete and utter darkness. The craziest part is how it seemed I had superhuman hearing and could hear everything around me. It was to the point where I could hear a conversation across the longest hallways. I couldn't talk as my vocal cords had swelled, although my emotions were able to remain in a super calm state. I felt at peace. It didn't take me long to start being able to communicate, but when I did, my voice was so high-pitched I thought I was a chipmunk. Talk about hilarious. My brother started talking to me and asked if I knew what happened. I told him that "the school blew up." He continued by saying that someone had shot me. The news didn't come as a big surprise to me as I knew something had happened. I just wasn't clear on precisely what occurred. I asked if anybody else was injured. Sadly, one of my friends was also hurt, yet she was already back home after her hospital stay. Bubba then asked me if I knew who did it. I was trying extremely hard to think back. Still, all I could remember was falling to the floor, completely blind, trying to get up and help many other people who I thought were injured by the "bomb" at the time before "passing out," which is when my heart stopped. He told me the shooter was Callum. My mind started to race as the few Callums I know are amazing kids. When he said the shooter's last name, Milton, my heart rate went through the roof. This guy is one of the last people I would have expected to do something like this.

I was somewhat angry as I figured they had to have the wrong guy. Yet, no matter how unbelievable this is, it was actually him. I was still utterly shocked as Callum was among the smartest, sweetest kids in the school. He was the guy we knew who was going to an Ivy League university after high school. Callum always had the biggest smile on his face, leading many people to believe he was the happiest kid on the planet. The two of us partnered up quite often in our honor's English class with Mrs. Peacock. I enjoyed partnering with him because he usually taught me what we needed to learn in that class as I could understand him so well, or so I thought.

After a while, my emotions settled to where my recovery could continue. I attempted to drink some water. Small sips were all that was possible to get down because I'd quickly start to choke. It was like learning how to drink again. The next day, water became pretty easy to swallow, so I started trying to eat the nugget ice. It was a little hard to get those down, but I managed. Over the next few days, eating a little ice cream was possible, and it was collectively tasty and liberating. The next challenge was the fact that my jaw would only open a couple of centimeters, which meant trying to eat anything larger than a french fry at most was quite tricky, if not impossible, at that moment. Throughout the week or two, while being sedated, fifty pounds or so were off the scale, so it was time I got back to eating some real food as opposed to what the tube was pumping into my belly. We started to pry open my jaw with an incredible tool, even though it didn't feel awesome. A few more days passed, and I was able to eat some small portions of food. I got out of bed and walked along the hall with a walker, trailed by my IV pump and nurse, Greyson. Speaking of Greyson, I knew exactly what he looked like even though I had never seen him before, and it was all because of that dream I had seen him in while under sedation. We successfully made it back to my bed after that seemingly extensive journey due to all of the muscle strength my body lost during the lengthy duration of time laying in the hospital bed.

My recovery was going pretty smoothly and quite exceptional, considering the initial damage to my body. The recovery progressed significantly quicker than any doctor had expected. I could eat, speak, and move around quite a bit, not to mention the fact that I was still alive. Medicine can't explain how I am alive today, but God can! This specific phrase continuously went through my head, and it's one I'll stand by every day moving forward. I have always had a spiritual faith, but the fact that I had died just a couple of weeks ago and was not only living but healing at such a rapid pace was indeed a miracle. I had honestly healed so fast that the doctors were already making plans to transport me by ambulance to the pediatric rehabilitation center in Dallas. One of the days before my transfer to the rehab center, my family helped me to dress into actual clothes as opposed to my usual hospital gown and walked me to another part of the hospital. While walking into a new room, I heard a large group of people yell, "Suprise!" Many of my other family members and close friends had come to visit me to show that they have been cheering and continue to cheer me on throughout my recovery. Reconnecting with people from back home felt liberating, and this moment undoubtedly brought a new source of strength into my body. It wasn't long after this surprise party before the doctors cleared me to load into the ambulance and head off to Dallas.

My dad was able to join me on the ride. As we were going down the road, we would have some short conversations as I was in and out of sleep. During one of the times when my brain was conscious, I was intrigued by the pellet that was right at the surface of the skin directly above my eyebrow. I started to pick at it and continued to do so for quite a while. Then, the small piece of metal popped out. I handed it over to my dad, and he asked me, "What is this?" my finger then pointed toward the area where I'd pulled it out. His next question was, "Did you just pull a pellet out of your face?" I smiled enormously big and started to laugh as I could only imagine the look on his face. The ambulance began to slow down and come to a stop. The medical transport team began to unload me from the ambulance and take me inside the rehabilitation center.

It was late at night, so I was ready for a good night's

rest. Part of my regular nightly routine at this point in time was a prayer for the healing of my body, my family, the shooter, his family, and anyone throughout my community who had been either directly or indirectly affected. My prayers always concluded by asking the Lord to fill the hospitals and rehab centers with His presence and asking that He and my niece hold my hand to help me drift into sleep. It never failed that every night, I would feel the warm sensation of a small hand resting on mine while feeling the hand of Jesus on the top of my head. As soon as I could feel their hands while snuggling my niece's tiny bear that her momma B brought for me, sleep was the most peaceful place for rest and healing. Immediately as I woke up the next morning, it was go time. The plan included multiple sessions of physical and mental rehabilitation, considering the damage to my body and the trauma to my brain. The first stop was with the psychologist. She started to ask me various questions to see what I remembered from the day of the shooting and evaluate how it affected me. As my brain attempted to reflect back to that day, I shared with her everything I could recall up until I lost consciousness. She began evaluating my recollection of general facts to see if I had lost any memory in relativity to the world we are living in. The question was, "Who is the President of the United States?". I quickly responded with "George Lopez," and although my vision was gone, I could almost see the angry look on her face as I laughed hysterically and said, "Just kidding. It's Barack Obama." In all fairness, I was only attempting to lighten the mood. I'm not sure how well I did with that, though.

As the day went on, it was time for physical therapy. We entered a room with lots of noise and soft mats everywhere. The therapist took me to a spot where she explained an obstacle course made of mats, and I had to find my way through it. It was tricky because the muscles that were once there were no longer a thing, and my bones were more stiff than a baseball bat. The therapist grabbed my hand, trying to help me over one of the mats. She just happened to grasp the hand that had the giant blister on it from where my vein exploded back on the helicopter a couple of weeks ago. I tried so hard not to cry, yet the pain was excruciating. It was not the first nor the last time that would happen, though.

We wrapped up physical therapy, and it was time for me to get back to my room to rest. After a quick nap, I woke up and started feeling around the top of my head, where the surgeon used staples to close up the incision they had made at the hospital for a tube. It felt like something wet, so I asked my family to call the nurse. When a nurse came in, I told her, "My head is leaking brain juice." The doctor walked through the door shortly after and believed I was going crazy, saying that it was normal and should stop soon. The next day, my head was still leaking brain juice, and when the doctor came back to look a second time, he had a transport team take me to the nearest hospital. As it turns out, I was right. The surgeons had to take me back into the operating room to close up the incision properly. Being the location of the open wound, I had to have a spinal tap, where they insert a massive needle into your spine to suck up some of the spinal fluid and test it for any infection. Luckily, the results came back negative. However, the amount of pain I was in immediately after waking up was unbearable. Sitting straight up seemed impossible as it felt like a bus drove directly into my spine. Once approved for discharge from the hospital, the transport team loaded me back into the ambulance to make our return to the rehab center.

When we arrived, I was certainly ready for a nap. Naps have become quite normal for me over the past few weeks. My time continued with therapy, and as I looked back just over the past few days, I realized that my body was starting to feel a little better. My muscles allowed me to move around more without much assistance. It was almost time for my big eye surgery. I'm a little nervous about it because, depending on how well the surgeon does, I could be fully blind forever or possibly regain some of my vision. Time continued to fly past, which was exciting as we were one day closer to returning home. I had a good amount of improvement during the past week and a half at the rehab center, so they released me, and it had already come time for me to head back to the hospital for the procedure on my eyes. Before going into surgery, I had to take some pills to help calm the nerves. Not long after, I was in a deep sleep. From what felt like one second to the next, my eyes flung back open, and I had to return directly to a squint. My excitement blew through the roof now that I could see some light the second my eyes opened following the surgery. This result was a miracle to me as my vision was completely gone in both eyes over the past four weeks before this surgery. I looked over at my family, and it was like getting the best Christmas present in the world as I could now see their faces. My vision wasn't like it used to be, but I was thankful to have even a little vision. The ophthalmologist started to explain how they were not able to restore any vision in my left eye this time. However, my right eye was in pretty good shape, and 90% of my retina was still attached. As I was in the process of attempting to calm my excitement, the surgeon placed a bandage contact lens over my right eye to leave on during the healing process. This moment meant triumph was already in motion.

My family and I made our way out of the hospital. We drove to a place called the Ronald McDonald House, which is similar to a hotel yet structured for a long-term stay. This location is where my family was staying while I was between the rehab center and the hospital. It was a place where families who had children receiving medical care could go to stay at no cost or an optional nightly donation because of the long duration of time away from home. On the way, we stopped and grabbed some food to take back to the room. After lunch, we went into the lobby area, where there were tons of cool activities they had set out for the kids there. I was a big fan of arts and crafts, so my sister guided me to a table full of origami paper. A really sweet lady who was part of the staff came up to me and guided my hands to teach me how to make a paper crane. We then shifted over to playing this cool game where you put these little rings on a platform and launch them into the air to land and make a row before the other player. I was having so much fun. Nighttime quickly approached, and after a couple of naptime visits back to the room, my family took me down to the lobby again for a surprise. I sat in this extremely comfy chair, and then I heard a person walk up to the left side of me.

As I turned in that direction, a man said, "Hi, Nathaniel! My name is Jason Garrett, Head Coach of the Dallas Cowboys. How are you?" I was completely shocked as the Head Coach of my favorite NFL team had come to visit me. He brought me a ton of merch with a signed football by all the team players. Coach Garrett brought an extra ball so we could play catch in the lobby. Thankfully, I had some of my vision back, so I could at least see where the ball was. He was one of the nicest guys I had ever met, leaving me with an experience I will never forget. Before he left, he handed me sideline tickets for my family and me to attend a game when I entered a state of complete recovery. Talk about a big score! Then, it was time for a good night's rest.

As soon as my body rolled out of bed the following day, my dad and I headed down to the kitchen, where he cooked us up some chorizo and egg burritos, one of my favorite breakfast meals. Once the food was ready, we returned to the room to eat while getting ready for the day. My mom's phone rang, and it sounded like they were trying to be a little sneaky. She stepped out into the hallway to take a few different phone calls, returned to the room, put the phone on speaker, and handed it over to me. What I heard next put me in shock yet again. "Hey Nathaniel, this is Derek Jeter with the New York Yankees. How are you feeling?" I was so amazed that my all-time favorite MLB player was talking to me. As I sat there in awe of all the people reaching out to show their support, I realized just how much more I was ready to push myself to become my absolute best and make an impact on other people. Before I knew it, the time had come to return home and work to finish out the rest of my recovery, as much as possible anyway. We got in the truck and drove back down to Lubbock, where I had a checkup with one of my doctors the following day. We arrived at the hotel and settled in to get some rest. I woke up bright and early, still filled with excitement, which led to me no longer falling back to sleep. Not only am I still adjusting to having some of my vision back, but I am also headed back home today for the first time in over five weeks.

After getting ready and eating a quick breakfast, my parents, sister, and I headed to the eye clinic for my post-op checkup. The doctor started to test my vision using various prescription lenses to analyze which lens would help me see the most miniature letters best. After about fifteen minutes, we found a lens that worked well. It didn't allow me to see perfectly by all means, yet I could see even better, and that's a satisfactory start for me. Before we left, the doctor noted the glasses prescription I needed. We needed to take the records to an optician and get some glasses. In the meantime, he had gifted the lens to me so I could take it wherever I went until I could get my glasses. Having the lens with me constantly is exactly what I did. Everywhere I went, so did my lens. The hardest part was when I would set it down somewhere and forget where I put it. It was even worse when we were riding in the truck, and it would fall into the small spaces between the seats. It was only the first day with the lens, so I tried to ease up on myself. I was ready to get on the road, as home was just a few hours away. As usual, I took my nap on the trip over to Roswell. Deep sleep is an understatement for that nap. However, my sister woke me up, telling me to get my shoes on as there was another surprise up the road not too far ahead of us. As the truck stopped on the side of the road, the windows rolled down, and a few men started talking to me. There were quite a few first responders, including police officers, sheriff's deputies, and paramedics, who had driven to the outskirts of town to escort me home. A man from the local car dealership also brought out a brand-new truck for us to ride into town with. I quickly, yet carefully, felt my way into the passenger seat of the new truck, and we were back on the road to Roswell.

As we reached the city limits, the windows rolled

down again, and I heard cheering coming from every direction. The entire city of Roswell lined the street from the second we hit town all the way to my front doorstep. Let me tell you, that was a pretty good distance for the small town of Roswell. As we pulled up to my house, there were even more people out there with tons of signs, balloons, and anything else you could think of to celebrate. News reporters from all over the state joined us in this celebration, asking my family, friends, and me various questions about our journey back home after being away from home for five weeks and three days. It was such an incredible experience to have so many people from my community welcome me home. It reassured me that I continue to have many good things and many great people to fight for. After we settled back into the house, a few people came in to check on me and see how I was doing. As time passed, I was in and out of sleep.

The next morning, I got ready as someone extra special was coming to visit. I heard the doorbell ring, and a few different people soon entered. As one of them approached me on the couch, she said, "Hi, Nathaniel! My name is Governor Susanna Martinez." My excitement at this point was uncontrollable. So many great things are happening with an endless amount of support. I can't explain how truly blessed I am. The Governor of New Mexico was literally sitting on the couch right next to me, seeing how I was doing. I later found out that she had also visited me in the hospital after making a stop at the middle school where the shooting happened. She then invited me to the legislative session to help be a voice for a policy that would begin to move school safety in a new direction.

Positively unforgettable experiences flowed like a rapid river, and I prayed to God, giving thanks for every single minute of it as nothing is possible without Him. Thankfully, most, if not all, students could return to school. There was no telling how many of them were still struggling on the inside, much less how it was affecting them on the outside, though. I was still recovering at home, yet there were some different homework assignments that I would do with my sister or my teacher, who would come over to the house. Speaking of that teacher, she is actually the teacher who was by my side the day of the shooting, along with the security guard. After we finished some assignments, especially those that were preparing me for state testing so I could get to eighth grade, we would have some detailed discussion of what happened the day of the incident. These are the times when I would find out specifics on how the shooter quickly entered the gym, dropped the bag, and fired the three shorts before anyone could do anything to stop it. Even learned how much I was bleeding on the ground that day and how she was having to scoop the blood out of my mouth to stop me from choking on it. Then, my heart stopped, and I was dead for seven to eight minutes until the paramedics were able to enter and take over. That's when I started gasping for air again. I discovered many other microscopic details of that day throughout various conversations I had with her and many other people who were in the gym when the shooting took place. It made me realize just how bad the scene looked from a visual perspective that day. We were able to finish all the assignments for the remainder of the semester, which quickly came to an end.

As a way to celebrate the end of the school year along with all of the things many students had to overcome in order to finish out the semester after returning back to school following the shooting, there was an extraordinarily awesome party we had out on the football field with tons of water balloons. Some of my friends called me over where they had a slingshot. They handed me the largest water balloon they could find and helped me to load it into the sling. I got a good grip on the handle, pulled my entire body down to the ground, and launched it into the air. My luck was that the balloon just happened to land on a girl that I genuinely liked. Thankfully, she found it to be quite hilarious and not in a sarcastic type of way. Time continued to speed by, and it was officially summer break. That said, this meant it was time for the journey to continue.

CHAPTER FOUR
TURNING THE PAGE

*"Hardships often prepare ordinary
people for an extraordinary destiny."*
– C.S. Lewis

In the State of New Mexico, we have this incredible Minor League Baseball team called the Albuquerque Isotopes. It was their season's opening night, and they invited Kaylani and me to throw the first pitch in the presence of the LA Dodgers' legendary Tommy Lasorta. The Isotopes gifted us with our own jerseys with our names on them and everything. It was indeed a night to remember.

As soon as we returned home, it was time to get started on my state testing. I would meet Mrs. Armbruster in her classroom at Berrendo, where we could project the exam in a magnified view on the smartboard. She would give me the time I needed in order to complete each of the questions and submit my answers effectively. There were a few different sessions we had to go through over a couple of days. I was able to finish and perform well above the required score in order to advance to eighth grade.

Then came more doctor's appointments. We had to travel up to Lubbock once a month at minimum for check-ups. It had become a pretty regular thing ever since I got home back in February. I would have to see a few different eye doctors for my retina and cornea, along with getting updated prescriptions for my enormously large eyeglasses. I'd also visit with my neurosurgeon to check on my brain. My dermatologist is another I'd see quite often to lighten my scars and cure this awful cystic acne I started to get due to the high amount of lead that continues to flow through my body from all the pellets still inside of me. I had to get my blood drawn every two weeks to check my lead levels. During the times it was above a certain level, I would once again have to take a two-week dose of that nasty, rotten-smelling medicine I was taking while I was in the hospital in order to get my lead levels back down. Although, I am thankful this didn't happen as often as it used to. My body had actually begun to stabilize quite a bit at this point. The only thing was I had a recurring calcium buildup on my right eye where they had taken out the lens—we as humans are often born with—a few months back. The calcium would cause my vision to get excessively blurry in a way that could not be corrected until I had the scraping done on my eye. Every three to six months, I would have an appointment with my ophthalmologist to conduct the scraping, where he would grasp a bladed tool and directly scrape the calcium off of my cornea. At the same time, I was completely awake with a speculum holding my eye open. The numbing drops helped a little, yet the pain was very much present. The only thing I could think about while lying on the operating table was how great I would be able to see in a couple of days following the scraping. As the procedure finished, the ophthalmologist placed a bandage contact lens on my eye, which would protect the treated portion during the healing process. As expected, my vision was noticeably better a couple of days later. During my post-op checkups, they would test my vision again to see how much it improved from the last time. After viewing the vision chart, I could tell it was much clearer than before the operation. It was now possible for me to even read a lower line with smaller letters, which is the line of letters I couldn't see at all during the visit before the procedure. It was so exciting to see clearly again. However, my vision had stabilized around 20/80 to 20/100, fluctuating between the two depending on how my eye wanted to work at the time.

As we returned home from my follow-up appointment, I had to mentally and spiritually prepare myself for the court hearing that was coming up in a few weeks, where I would have to sit in the same room as the shooter and share why I felt like he should receive the maximum sentence for what he did. That is all while surrounded by our families, friends, and many others throughout the community. As I sat down in front of the computer to begin typing out my letter that I would read before the court, I magnified the screen, changed the font size to 36pt, and started to think of what all I needed to say to truly leave a lasting impact which showed how serious the everlasting injuries truthfully are. After a lot of thought, I knew it didn't entirely matter what I said during the hearing, as my attendance in the courtroom would show how the injuries impacted my body physically, which spoke for itself. I began to type out the different sorts of things that I struggled with now as a result of my injuries. Remembering back to what my doctors told me, my life was now going to be completely different as I may never be able to drive or pursue particular careers in the future which required me to have perfect vision, or when I enter my adult life, I may never be able to have biological kids of my own. This news is undoubtedly a thing kids at my age shouldn't have to think about as we are still kids ourselves. I would surely mention much of that in the letter I typed up. Prayer was an absolute must for a little while as this is where seeking answers was found as to whether I was taking the right approach with this letter or not. It made sense for me also to think back to the person I once knew before he became a school shooter and tried to process why he would do something like this. My prayers were also for him, as he was now likely going to spend all of his teenage years in state custody. I wanted to make sure God was making moves in his life to help him recover and become a better person again like he was before any of the horrific thoughts that he acted upon entered his mind. As always, I gained a lot of clarity through prayer and was able to piece the final version of my letter together. I printed a copy and placed it into the folder we plan to take with us on the day of the sentencing. When I stepped back for a minute to think about the sentencing date, I quickly realized it was on my mom's birthday. I wasn't pleased about that as my mom now had to spend her birthday watching the sentencing of the kid who nearly killed her son. These were the only parts throughout this journey that would upset me because even though I forgave the shooter immediately after my brother told me who it was while I was in the hospital, the rest of my family understandably had a tough time coping with the fact that I was shot and nearly lost my life because of someone else's actions. Needless to say, time was still scrambling by while staying still simultaneously, and it had already come time for the day to convict the shooter for the crimes he committed.

As we woke up, we started getting ready, and we were all much quieter that morning than any other. Breakfast didn't feel necessary as our stomachs felt twisted in every different direction. We loaded into the car and made the drive over to the courthouse. As we entered the courthouse's general proximity, we saw vehicles parked bumper to bumper on every street in the area, which meant it was quite challenging to find a parking spot. Once we did, it was time to walk into the courthouse. As expected, tons of news reporters were there with all the cameras, trying to capture the story. I did my best to answer some of their questions beforehand as they were simply trying to do their job. Yet, it was genuinely hard for me as all I could think about was being in a room with the shooter and that the shooter was once a kid who I believed would never hurt a soul. As we entered the courtroom, we were able to sit in the very front of the gallery and wait as the lawyers, the courtroom staff, and, most importantly, the judge were all ready to go behind the scenes. The shooter was brought into the room wearing an orange jumpsuit in cuffs and placed in his seat beside his legal council. The judge then entered the courtroom, where we stood at the "All Rise" command from the bailiff. We sat down following the "Please Be Seated" request from the judge.

As we sat down, the court proceedings were quickly in order. We heard the charges proposed for the shooter and the possible outcomes of the sentencing. It came time to listen to the opening statements from the prosecuting and defense attorneys. Statements of evidence for the various investigations followed. One particular piece that brought out many of my heartbreaking emotions was when they read the journal the shooter had left in his room for his parents. Only a few days before the incident, the journal entries came into existence. In the first entry, Callum wrote that he was going to take a particular gun into his first-period class and shoot [the bully whose name appeared as written] in the shoulder to get him to turn around and then shoot him in the head. It followed that Callum did his research, and because of his age, he would only be in state custody until the age of 21. On the next day, he wrote that the gun was unable to be located, so instead, Callum was going to take a knife into his first-period class. During the pledge of allegiance on the morning announcements, he was going to stab [the bully] in the shoulder to get him to turn around and slice his throat to watch him die and suffer "ha-ha-ha." I was balling my eyes out at this point as I could not believe what this kid had written in the journal. What didn't surprise me was the name of who he said the bully was that he wanted to kill. The bully was the same guy I showed up at basketball tryouts before the incident who thought he was too good and always managed to be a jerk to a lot of people. For context, back to the journal, this second entry with the knife was the plan for when we returned to school that Monday after winter break, yet school was canceled that day due to the water break. The third and final journal entry reading occurred, which became the plan following the school cancellation on Monday. Callum knew it would be cold outside and that we would likely go inside the gym on Tuesday morning. Following the meticulous search of his house to find a weapon, he located the shotgun. As reflected in his final journal entry, Callum planned to saw off the stock end of the gun to fit it into his duffle bag, take the gun into the gym, and fire three random shots to get the point across that he was tired of being bullied. This plan seemed more effective for him as he could get it over with before risking someone stopping him with the bag. Following the journal reading, law enforcement stated all of what they located during their execution of the search warrants, where they found the saw used to cut off the stock end along with the shavings and the journal. It turns out there was also a post on Instagram Callum had shared the late night before the shooting, telling people not to go to school the next day because bad things were going to happen, yet very few people saw the post because of the timing.

Following the conclusion of the evidence portion, many of the witnesses had to give their own personal statements. When the attorney called my name to the stand to present my statement, fear tried to creep in, although it quickly vanished as I prayed on the way up there. Thankfully, the awesome courthouse facility dog and the extraordinary Pastor Troy—who brought me so much comfort—followed directly behind me. After concluding my statement, we returned to our seats, and it was just about time to hear the court's final decision following the recess. In the State of New Mexico, a minor cannot be prosecuted with premeditated murder. The only charges applicable due to those conditions consisted of three counts of battery with a deadly weapon and carrying a weapon on school grounds, resulting in the court deciding to proceed with sentencing the shooter to state custody, where he will remain until the age of 21 which is the maximum sentence possible, as noted by Callum in his journal. The court hearing adjourned momentarily after. As we exited the courtroom, all parties encountered a ton of news reporters once again who wanted to hear our thoughts on the sentencing outcome. I gave them some insight into what I thought and hoped that Callum would find his way back to God during the duration of his incarceration. A large group of people from the community decided to go for a nice lunch with my family and me to decompress from all the emotions we had just poured into the court hearing. It was nice to have most of our questions answered and begin to find a more clear sense of closure. Days went by, and life kept getting better as time passed. It was coming time to get back to school, which also meant summer was coming to an end, and indeed, it did.

CHAPTER FIVE
BLESSINGS IN THE BATTLE

*"A smooth sea never
made a skilled sailor."*
– Franklin D. Roosevelt

It's 6 am, and my alarm is going off again in an attempt to wake me up for school. While I did consider hitting the snooze button, I held back. My mind was already starting to race, thinking about all of the friends I was going to see again and how great it was going to be getting back to school. Then, the thought crossed my mind of how my safety, along with the safety of others, was going to be impacted. The question, "Could something as bad as the shooting happen again?" began to repeat in my head. All these negative thoughts came to a halt when I snapped that I simply needed to pray about it and ask for protection over all students and all schools across the nation. Once my prayer wrapped, I rolled out of bed and quickly made my way to the shower as I was determined to make today the best first day of school ever. With the usual routine of getting showered, dressed, and finishing up with breakfast, I was shockingly ready early, which was unusual. I would often walk out the door in a rush to either catch the bus or help my parents get to work on time after dropping me off. Last school year, I rode the bus every day unless I missed it, of course. This year, my parents and myself included, figured it would be best to at least start out the school year with them taking me to school.

As we drove up to the final stop of the drop-off lane, I paused for a moment and realized that I was fixing to walk into the school where I nearly lost my life. Plus, I was now walking in with impaired vision, which would soon bring additional challenges on top of what I had already figured out over the last few months. I got out of the car and gave my family a nice giant hug, then the real journey started. As I made my way down the halls, some people would nicely say, "Welcome back," some would come up to me quickly and share an exciting moment with me that I was back, and others who I could tell were a little more standoffish and gave some pretty dirty looks. I made it a point to be understanding of everybody's reactions no matter the result, though, because no matter how much we think we know people, everyone processes things in different ways. In all fairness, it has only been six months or so since the shooting happened, which is not very long for people to truly find healing. My hope stood that if people saw me returning to the same school where the shooting transpired, they would feel a sense of hope for their healing process as well.

While walking into first-period, I saw one of my best friends that I hadn't seen in a while. I made my way over to him, saying hi and asking how he was doing. His bare response consisted of, "Hey," and that's all. It somewhat hurt my feelings because I hadn't seen this guy in months. Thinking the best of people, it seemed safe to assume his reaction may have been because of fear as I now have some quite noticeable changes in appearance with the scars all over my head and face along with some Coke bottle eyeglasses. Needless to say, I went on with my day, and it became evidently better from that point forward. It was incredibly wonderful to reconnect with so many of my classmates and get to understand how they were doing after witnessing such a gruesome scene last school year. I felt blessed with the fact that I didn't visually encounter that whole situation as I believe that was one big part of getting a jumpstart to my healing process. My struggles did not consist of such things as visual flashbacks that would set me back. I hope to provide as much support, if not more, to my classmates as they and the community showed me. That biggest challenge was when it came to socializing, as it became clear to me my recognition of people was based solely on their voice rather than attempting to look at their faces. I could see enough to get around and not bump into people or objects, yet I couldn't see faces evidently enough to know who I was looking at. This challenge is one that I consider to be the most prominent, as I love to be social with people. However, I didn't want to walk up to someone thinking it was a specific person and then be wrong and make it a whole awkward situation, potentially causing someone else to feel uncomfortable. After the first few weeks, the people who didn't noticeably understand how I operated with my new vision now would think that I was ignoring them and walking by without saying hi to acknowledge the fact that they were there. On the other hand, people who knew how I operated would come up to me saying, "Hey, Nathaniel! It's [their name]," and we would start up some pretty memorable and remarkable conversations.

The next challenge was the lack of ability to see the content I was supposed to learn from in the classroom. No matter how close I sat to the board, seeing what was written or projected into it appeared impossible. No matter how close the books came to my face, I couldn't read a single word. After communicating this problem with my teachers, they attempted to work with me the best they could. Thankfully, there was an extraordinary woman who would be the one who did whatever it took to get me the tools and resources I needed to succeed in my education. Not long after returning to school, any printed content began getting enlarged to 18-24pt font. If the text size was not a factor that was possible to change, I had magnifying devices that could be used to assist me in seeing small content. Then, when my eye became too tired, I had devices that would read text and graphic elements to me, which were displayed on different pages. This technology was undoubtedly all thanks to Mrs. Romero, the extraordinary woman I mentioned earlier. I don't know what I would have done without her. Little did I know, the two of us would have a long journey of challenges to work through as time progressed, yet I knew she would always be there to support me along the way. I was significantly stubborn for quite a while, trying to adjust to using these assistive devices to help me see things better, yet she helped me understand how much easier my life would be if I utilized them. Of course, many other awesome people were doing great things for me behind the scenes to help me succeed, which I am more than grateful for. I wasn't sure who had done certain things for me, but their support never went unnoticed.

This enormous amount of support in my education is what kept me going, especially when it came to that kind of teacher every once in a while who had a problem revising these small extra things for me, such as making a printed copy larger for me to see. With one specific teacher, this became quite normal. Whenever I needed any type of accommodation for the assignments, she would have a problem with it and make it a point to have some very negative emotions followed by enraged commentary about it. These encounters reached a point where I felt it was time to speak up and confront her about it. While making my walk to her desk to have this conversation quietly, out of what little respect I had left for her, she decided to speak much louder for the whole class to hear and call me out that I was needy and would not be successful in life. My emotions became furious with what she had just said to me, so I felt it was only right to walk out of the class and find an administrator to talk about what happened. I made my way into the first administrator's office, which appeared to be available. I shared the words that the teacher said to me and followed with a request to be switched out of her class as I was not going to put up with her negativity and disrespect to me when my attitude had been nothing but nice and patient with her when it comes to my accommodations. There were times when she wouldn't enlarge my assignments. I would ignore her lack of abiding by my accommodations and use some of the assistive devices Mrs. Romero supplied for me. The Assistant Principal shared that we were too far into the semester to modify schedules. However, they would find a way to resolve these situations in that class. The worst part about it was the fact that I had this teacher for two periods every day. We worked things out so that I could go to a different class during those periods and have a teacher who didn't throw a fit every time they had to spend an extra minute or two in the printing room to make my assignments more legible.

Life was going great after that. At least until the day we had the first fire drill of the semester. As anticipated, we successfully made our way out past the school parking lot by properly evacuating everyone out of the building. When given permission for everyone to walk in and return to class, all of us students chitchatted with each other on the way in. A guy in front of me who is new to the school turns around and says, "Can you shut the f*** up already. I'm sick of people always catering to you". It threw me off as I had never even met this dude before, and he was coming at me like that. The few classmates around me quickly jumped in and had my back on this, which I greatly appreciated. Him, not so much.

As the day coasted onward, things kept getting weirder. The security guard knocked on the door and requested that I be pulled out of class and taken down to the office. When I walked over there, I saw sheriff's deputies and city police officers conversing. My curiosity spiked, and I became interested in what they were doing there. Nobody would tell me anything, and as I asked questions, they insisted on waiting until my parents arrived. After twenty minutes or so passed, I saw my parents and siblings walk in. They asked if I was alright and then taken into a conference room with the law enforcement officers. My thoughts were racing, thinking this could be something good or downright horrible. They talked for a long time in the conference room, and I was left in the other conference room down the hall, wondering what was happening. Finally, they came and asked me to go into the conference room they were in. When I entered, everyone in there asked me again if I was alright. My reply signified that I was fine yet still questioning what was happening. They asked if I had any recent bad encounters with anyone at the school. My brain started to wonder, trying to think as I couldn't remember right off, but then I remembered what had happened that morning with the new guy telling me to shut the f*** up even though I had already let that go. When I told them about that, they said an investigation was taking place at the school to determine a certain student's handwriting. Turns out, someone had written in one of the bathroom stalls their statement, which read, "I will finish off Nathaniel on 9-2-14". This information came as a surprise to me as my life is now under threat for who knows what reason and no telling who. There were a couple of students that the staff had called down to the office and were holding them to ask questions when their parents arrived. I saw one of the students they called down there as he walked by, and I knew him to be one of the most awesome guys at that school. Though we all know my history of knowing a nice guy and what that turned out to be. The law enforcement officers kept all of us there for quite a while. The final bell had already rang for everyone—except us—to be released and head home or wherever else the world may take them. It was already two hours past the end of the school day. The officers updated us that they had found who had written that note on the bathroom stall and the next steps they were taking to deal with that situation. To nobody's surprise, it was the guy who told me to shut up earlier that day after the fire drill. It turns out he was angry at the reality that I was allowed to take my phone out during class, which would only be taken out to use the flashlight, allowing me to see pages better. He also believed I was getting special treatment for not having to be in class, which were the times my counselor would take me out of class to learn about new assistive technology that could help me see things better. Due to the severity of what was a literal death threat, he was no longer able to return to that school, and no telling what happened to him from that point. All I knew was that I was ready to move on with life once again and not allow things like that to hold me back.

Life went on, and I gradually adjusted to new learning strategies little by little while still adapting to impaired vision processes. As I mentioned earlier, my social circle was slightly smaller because of my struggle with seeing faces. The best part was my best friends—aside from the one in my first class that I mentioned earlier—and I were all still sitting at the same lunch table, making many more great memories just like we did the semester before the shooting. That was one place where I truly felt like things were back to normal, at least as normal as it could be anyway. The first semester back was already halfway over, and things were going super amazing overall. Especially when my brother asked me to be his best man at his wedding. He doesn't know this—unless he ever reads the book—but after he asked me and I said yes, I had to go into another room to cry it out for a minute as I couldn't control how excited and honored I was to be his best man.

A few weeks after that, my parents had planned a trip for us to travel to Dallas and use those sideline tickets

Coach Garrett had gifted me while I was at the rehab center back in February. Once we arrived in Dallas, we unloaded all of our luggage at a favorably superior hotel and quickly laid down to get some rest after that long eight-hour drive. As we woke up, it was time to get ready with all of our fan gear and head over to the stadium. When we arrived and located the area the staff requested us to enter, we were greeted by one of their tour guides. They took us on an awesome tour of the stadium, where I got to see all the locker rooms and film rooms where the players get prepped and suited up for each game. I even went out on the field through the tunnel where the players run out right before kick-off. The tour guide led us to the sideline, where we could stand during pre-game and see all the players warm up. All the players, including my favorites, ran by and high-fived me. Right after, I saw the outline of a man running up to me quickly. As he got closer, I realized who it was because of the excellent color of his hair I had seen in pictures, and he gave me the biggest hug ever. It was, in fact, Coach Garrett. He was so happy to see me, and I was even more happy to actually see him with my eye this time, being that I was completely blind when I first met him during his visit to the rehab center. We had an awesome conversation before he walked back out to the field for the final game prep. My parents and I made our way up to the seats where we had a premium view. The game, the tour, and all of the awesome people I was able to meet was an experience I will never forget.

Once I returned back home, the winter break bolted past like many others as they seemed to go by even faster each year. I was most excited about the fact that the wedding was already happening in a couple of months. Once my brother and his fiancée—who I've considered my sister-in-law for the past 9 years that they have been together—decided on the tuxedos and dresses the groomsmen and bridesmaids in their wedding were going to wear, I was fitted for my suit, and I felt like a billion bucks. It was time to make a trip to my excellent barber—who has been one of my brother's best friends ever since I've been alive—for the freshest fade I ever had so I could be looking good for the big day. The wedding day was already here, and it was even more cool that it was Valentine's Day. What better day to get married than the day of love, right? I rubbed a palm full of gel in my hair, slipped on my suit, and it was game time. I walked down the aisle with the amazing aunt of the Bride, her Maid of Honor, and then reached my spot beside the Groom. As the rest of the bridesmaids and groomsmen made their way down the aisle, I couldn't help but glance at my brother repeatedly to make sure I saw his face once he first saw his Bride in her wedding dress. Surely enough, the song they chose together started to play. She appeared around the corner, and he nearly lost it, even though he may tell you otherwise. It didn't take me long after that to do the same. The happiness and joy within the church was extraordinary. As soon as we made the transition to the reception, I was ready to dance. My nerves often got the best of me at first, especially since I had a portion of the best man speech to give with his best friend, who was deservingly the other best man. Yet, once I get out on the dance floor, good luck getting me off. It was indeed so that I was on the dance floor all night, and my feet made sure to pay me back for being on them like that for so long. No matter what my feet tried to tell me, I made sure that we all had an amazing night to remember. I was also glad that the next day was a Sunday, which meant I had some time to relax my feet before going back to school. Once that time came, I was excited and terrified at the same time as high school is so close, yet how in the heck was it already time for me to transition into high school? Like seriously, where has time gone?

CHAPTER SIX
BEYOND THE CLASSROOM

*"Life begins at the end
of your comfort zone."
– Neale Donald Walsch*

Freshman year came in pretty hot. I couldn't believe that high school was already here, which meant I had four years until it was time for me to start college and become a whole adult. I was still upset with the fact that I couldn't play sports anymore, so I had to find something else to fill my time. On the first day of school, a girl greeted me as soon I walked through the door who had huge fluffy hair and such high energy that I thought she might have just drank twenty cups of coffee. I was here for it because it was clear she would be one of my good friends. She invited me to attend a meeting after school to learn about an extremely incredible student organization, and they would have ice cream. Honestly, I only heard ice cream at that moment, and this was a way to start making new friends. The school day went by as we did the usual first-day tasks of getting the syllabus with the supplies we would need to buy and bring to class. As the final bell rang, I made my way to the classroom where the meeting was taking place. I saw a ton of Juniors and Seniors there. It was pretty intimidating, yet in the corner was the fluffy hair that I could recognize anywhere. I could feel her excitement as soon as I turned down the hallway.

After signing into the meeting, I went over to sit by her. The meeting convened quickly, and the advisor started sharing what this student organization was all about and why we should consider becoming a member of Business Professionals of America, also known as BPA. This opportunity seemed like something good to do, as I was ready to get sports off my mind as that was no longer an option. Over the next few weeks, the school year was going pretty great, and so was my involvement with BPA along with everything else I wanted to join, including Family, Career, and Community Leaders of America (FCCLA) and Mathematics, Engineering, Science, Achievement Club (MESA Club). Mrs. Romero was still a very influential advocate for me in my education as I transitioned from middle school into high school. There were still a few of those teachers here and there who would have a problem making the accommodations of making the text bigger, enlarging the graphic content on the pages, or giving me extra time on assignments that took me a little longer to complete. Yet, I also had many excellent teachers who would go out of their way to ensure my accommodations were taken care of while assuring they provided all the necessary tools I needed to be exceptional in their class. If any of the teachers slipped up, not only did Mrs. Romero work with me in high school, I had an additional team of transformational advocates who continued to help change the game of my education to make sure I did the absolute best that I could do such as Ms. Grant, Ms. Gallegos, and Ms. Rivas. I had every bit of academic support needed and beyond. The amount of appreciation I have for all of these remarkable women is unexplainable. The support received from our Principal, Mr. Lovett, was phenomenal, as he was always willing to help me succeed in everything I did.

On one of the morning announcements, I heard that there were golf tryouts. I wanted to know if this was something I could do with approval from my doctors, as golf is indeed a sport with no contact unless you get hit by a golf ball, of course. I went ahead and decided to take on golf as well to at least get some sort of sport back into my life. After making the team and attending the first few practices, I liked it, although it wasn't the same as baseball, basketball, and football, which are all the sports that I loved. I wouldn't quit as I am not a quitter, so finishing the season was a priority.

When it came to BPA, I had a regional conference coming up, which is the first competition that determines which competitors advance on to state. I got a good amount of preparation in before the conference by doing a few various practice tests on the specific competitive event I chose for the year. Then, it came time to get set and take the exam. I decided to compete in banking and finance as I figured it would be something good to take on in preparation for life after high school.

One thing I am even more excited about than anything else at the time is the birth of Bubba and B's TWINS. The morning we expected B to go into labor, my mom was under the impression that I was going to school. I started crying that morning because my heart felt shattered at the fact that I wouldn't be at the hospital when my niece and nephew were born. Thankfully, after crying long enough, I went with the rest of my family to the hospital. We spent a very long day in the waiting room, where I decided to do as much schoolwork as possible on my laptop. However, when everyone else thought I was doing schoolwork, I was researching how to be the world's best uncle. Later that afternoon, when we received word about the twins arriving soon, I dropped everything I was doing, waiting as patiently as I could on the edge of my seat for them to let us go back and see them. After what felt like weeks in the waiting room, the hospital staff finally peaked around the corner and said they were ready for us. My feet hit the ground quickly while entering an immediate speed walk, where my parents then asked me to slow down. An attempt was made to respect their wishes. However, I couldn't help it, so I slowed down a little, but not much. As soon as I stepped into the room, seeing my brother with Baby A and my sister-in-law with Baby B, my heart fell through the floor with absolute love for these kids. Especially when I held Baby B, as all she could do was look into my eye—since I can only see out of one, haha—with the most adorable smile I had ever seen. Seeing B and my brother with these babies after trying for so many years, my heart was literally glowing inside of me. Sadly, we had to go home a few hours later for some rest. I was still pretty excited about my competition coming up, though. The only thing is I was more excited to get back home to see the twins.

At the regional conference, I was competing against several other people. I was a little nervous, yet I went into the testing room, did the best I could on the test, and placed first, allowing me to advance to state in a couple of months. After returning to school, it was time to finish up the first semester of ninth grade, followed by a nice winter break. The family and I had our traditional meal made by my dad. It was convincing to say that the meals tasted better every year he made them. We also had some awesome presents to open and many more to give as I had a three-month-old niece and nephew who are twins to celebrate this Christmas. It was certainly something to celebrate as I was so happy for my brother and sister-in-law for finally getting their much-deserved blessing of such adorable babies after everything they had been through together. As usual, the break came to a quick end, and it was time to get back to school and finish out freshman year.

As soon as I returned to school, it was surely go time to prepare for the State Leadership Conference in Albuquerque. The conference was not far away. We only had about five weeks until the competition. I continued to use previous years' practice tests to study and ensure I stayed within the sixty-minute time frame allotted to complete the test on competition day. It was also time for me to start preparing my business suit. After all the practice tests, suit purchases, and packing, I was finally ready to head to state. When my chapter and I got to the hotel and conference center, we unloaded all of our luggage, checked in at the front desk, and took our stuff up to the rooms. We then were able to sneak away and have some fun at a super fun trampoline park, followed by a great-tasting dinner.

The next day was competition day, and I was nervous but excited at the same time. I suited up that morning and was ready to give this competition my absolute best. We first had to attend the opening session where the State Officers elected by the members who were voting delegates last year would share conference highlights and then hear the speeches for the members who were now candidates to be elected for State Office the following year. I was amazed by the courage these student members had to get up on stage in front of so many other students and give a one to two-minute speech as to why the voting delegates should vote for them to serve as State Officers, representing New Mexico BPA. I was so impressed and admired by what the current and potential newly-elected State Officers were doing that I knew I wanted to do something like that one day. After arriving at my competition room, it was time to take the test. The content wasn't enlarged, but we obtained approval to take my phone into the room and help me magnify the text with the camera. The questions were quite tricky, yet I had to reflect on all the preparation I did with the practice tests. I kept looking at the time, and it felt like every minute passed in a second. With only a minute left, I was able to complete the test without going over time and being disqualified. I made my way out of the room. Then, I went to a few different leadership workshops with some of my chapter members while others competed in their competitive events.

The conference went by fast as well, and it was time for the awards session. This part of the conference is when we found out who placed in the top ten in each competition and who the top three to five were who would go to nationals. I patiently waited for the announcement of my competitive event name while celebrating my fellow chapter members who had placed. The announcer called out my event name and started to call up the top ten finalists to the stage soon after. He had already called eight names, meaning only two spots were left. I was happy to hear my name being the next one called, and I made my way up to the side of the stage. As the State Officers directed us onto the stage, we stood waiting to hear the top three who made it to nationals. The announcer called three names, and sadly, mine wasn't one. I was proud to have placed in the top ten during my first year in the organization.

As we returned back to school, I was now able to focus primarily on school again and wrap up the golf season as well. I finished my first year of high school feeling good about it, and then summer came. It was time that I started trying to make some money while also building professional skills that I could use to start building my resume. With the help of my excellent vocational rehabilitation counselor, I secured an internship-style job with the Bureau of Land Management, where I learned all about oil and gas wells and some cool wildlife and aviation facts within southeast New Mexico. Overall, it was a great experience as my first job, and I am excited to make my own money now.

Sophomore year came up fast, and it was time for me to return to school. Back to school also meant going back to the academic struggles and student organizations, which helped me understand that I am my own enemy in the sense that the only limits I have are those I set for myself. I had a smooth transition into sophomore year. Things were going great. In fact, things were going so great to the point where I knew I wanted to expand my leadership journey, as I believed I had the potential to become whatever and whoever I set out to become. I remembered from last year's New Mexico BPA State Leadership Conference that I felt inspired by how the former State Officers got up onto the stage with the confidence they had to speak to hundreds of other students. While looking back on that, I realized a challenge was coming on.

Back then, I used to find challenges with how great of an athlete I was. Now, I challenge myself with the question of how great of a speaker I can be and how great of a leader I might become. I began to envision what I could be and who I may become in the future. That is when I decided to move forward in submitting my application to become a candidate and run for state office. The part that began to worry me was that I have never been in front of an audience any larger than the twenty to thirty people in a classroom while giving a presentation. Now, I had the opportunity to speak in front of hundreds of other students in a convention center with all the attention on me while sharing why I deserve their vote. It was time that I stopped worrying about all the things that could go wrong because I needed to shift my focus to how I could create a great speech that would bring a significant impact. And so it began. As I started to think about an overall theme for my campaign, I wanted to ensure that it stood for something meaningful to help tie all of my objectives together if elected into state office. The words from one of my favorite athletic apparel brands continued to pop into my head, as this is something I always tell myself when I am procrastinating or doubting myself. That is when I decided my campaign theme would be precisely that of those words, "Just Do It." Nike is a brand that I have worn for years when playing sports or even for my everyday outfits. I decided to no longer let the sadness of not playing sports hold me back and instead allow it to fuel the great things I do moving forward.

The conference was right around the corner, and I felt

good about all the campaign material I had put together. The only challenge now was the fact of me not being
able to clearly see the script that I had put together for my
campaign speech. I knew there was the option to enlarge
the text however big that enabled me to read it. Although,
I didn't want to be that guy standing behind a podium,
looking down, reading from a piece of paper. Much of my
preparation consisted of practicing the speech to get the
overall concept down. My only thought now was to mem-
orize the speech entirely so I could break away from reading a script and be free to step out from behind that podium to own the stage like it was mine. It was already time
for state, and I knew it was fixing to be go time as soon as
we arrived at the hotel in Albuquerque. Indeed, it was.

Once I got my bags and campaign materials up to my
room, I changed into my suit in preparation for the opening session that night, when all the candidates would get
up onto the stage to give their campaign speeches. I was
extremely nervous, but knowing that I had done all the
preparation possible up to this point, it was time to go out
there and do my absolute best. I gathered together all of
my campaign materials to take them downstairs and set
up my table for the campaign rally. The materials included
a poster with various pictures of me in action, in addition
to some chocolate Nike sneakers that complimented my
slogan. As soon as we finished the rally setup, my campaign manager and I walked into the conference room,
where we saw the current State Officers rehearsing their

portions of the script for the opening session. The state staff directed all of us candidates and our campaign managers over to the reserved seating area. Very quickly, the doors open, and hundreds of members storm in to fill all the seats in the room.

Then, when we hear the rap of the gavel, it means the opening session is now in order. The current State Officers presented a variation of conference highlights and information about what will be happening throughout the duration of the event. Then, they announced that it was time to hear the candidates' campaign speeches. A couple of candidates were called up to the stage before me, which I was thankful for as it allowed me to get a little less anxious until I heard my name called to the stage. I settled my crazy emotions and knew that I was fixing to give it my all, so it was time for me to walk up onto the stage with all the confidence I could possibly have within me. I successfully made it up the three steps onto the stage, grabbed the microphone off the podium, and made my way to center stage. I knew it was my cue to begin, so I took off with it. I made "eye contact" with the audience while walking to different parts of the stage to address everyone in the room. And by "eye contact," I mean me looking at the top of their heads as my vision is awful, and that's about all my one eye could see anyway, haha. I found that to be a perk for me. When the time came for the middle portion of my speech, I had to stop suddenly, looking a little lost, as it felt impossible to remember what else I was supposed to say.

It felt like an eternity, yet it was only five or ten seconds. After that awkward moment—at least of what I felt to be uncomfortable—it all came rushing back to me.

I successfully wrapped up my speech within the two-minute timeframe. It was such a relief as soon as I stepped off the stage, as that was the part I was most worried about. Once the State President closed the session, we entered the room where we had set up the table for the campaign rally. When it was time, the doors opened to let the voting delegates in. This rally is where they had the opportunity to view all of the campaign materials each of us candidates had created and ask us any questions related to our campaign and our goals for the organization if we were elected. The rally went on for a reasonable amount of time. I was happy about it as it felt like I had finally broken out of my shell and could be social in an entirely different way than what I am used to. As soon as we finished with the campaign rally, the voting delegates had the final task of placing their votes. At that point, we all had to wait until the end of the closing and awards session of the conference to find out if we got elected into state office or not.

The next thing I had to focus on was my competition. I was also giving a speech for my competition this year. A lot of preparation was executed for that as well. The only thing was that it felt like I didn't prepare enough since I was more focused on my campaign speech for a good reason. The next day, I entered the competition room during my scheduled time and presented my five to seven-minute speech on business and non-profit organizational structure. I felt confident throughout my presentation, although I wished my head hadn't looked down at my notes so often. After walking out of the room, I knew that my best presentation skills were shown to the judges during that speech. I was ready to hear their feedback from the judging rubrics following the conference. I went to a few different leadership workshops throughout the remainder of the day until it was time for us to head back up to our rooms and get comfortable for the fun time we had scheduled to get out of the hotel and be our full-on kid selves for a while. It was great to escape the professional feeling world for a bit and have a good dinner. When we returned to the hotel, I was certainly ready for bed.

As soon as I woke up for the final day of the conference, I sat in silence to breathe and reflect on what I had just accomplished over the last couple of days. I realized that I had just given my very first speech in front of a large number of people. I realized I could be social in a different type of way, which helped me become more confident in myself. I also learned that no matter the result of what I placed in my competition and whether or not I am elected into office, it was clear I was on track to no longer create any limits for myself. I was now on the way to the unstoppable version of me with big dreams for the future. Then, after standing up out of bed, tall and proud, I started getting ready. When we walked downstairs and into the main conference room, we found an empty section for our whole school's chapter to sit while listening to a great soundtrack to get pumped up for the final session. As soon as the session started, we saw a cool reflection video with tons of pictures taken during the conference. Then, the announcer shared that it was time to find out who had placed in each competition. There were a lot of competitive events, so I had to pay close attention to hear the announcement of my competitive event. After about forty-five minutes, I heard the announcer say, "And your finalists for Prepared Speech..." which is when I gripped my seat, hoping to hear my name. Ten names would be called to the side of the stage. After hearing the first five or six, my body began to feel all the senses of worry, thinking I didn't place high. The announcer called the ninth name, and it still wasn't me. I gripped my seat even tighter, and it was at that point when I heard "Nathaniel Tavarez from Goddard High School." Out of excitement, I ran to the side of the stage to get my finalist medal. They then directed us finalists onto the stage to hear who the top three competitors were. Sadly, I didn't place in the top three, although I am proud to have achieved being one of the top ten in the state. The announcer called the final competitive events, and then it was time to find out who would serve on the newly elected State Officer team. The announcer built excitement and momentum with the music playing loudly. His next words were, "And your first New Mexico BPA State Officer is... Nathaniel Tavarez!" I jumped out of my seat so quickly to head up onto the stage while the crowd shouted excitedly behind me. I felt so whole as it didn't seem my votes would be very high considering I stumbled on my speech halfway through yet was thankfully able to recover. I realized that those who voted were not judging me on how great I did in the speech but instead saw me as someone whose goals they believed in. The rest of the state officer team, who I would serve alongside this upcoming year, were called up, and we all joined in closely, ready to take on this next membership year together. The conference wrapped up, so I took all of my stuff downstairs to the truck, loaded it, and hit the road back home. Once I jumped in the truck and we took off, it was time to make a few phone calls to share with some important people that I am officially a 2017-2018 New Mexico BPA State Officer.

Once we arrived home, I thankfully had a good amount of time to rest and recharge for school the following week. On the first day back to school, I heard the great news of my election to the State Office in the morning announcements, which was super cool. Classes were going decently well, and I knew there were only a few months left until school was out for the summer. I worked much harder to ensure my grades were up to where they needed to be and guaranteed that I was doing good work on all my class projects. As always, the semester ended rather quickly, even though it collectively felt like forever. I was even more excited for the summer this time, though, because not only would it be my birthday, but it would also be my first training with the Career and Technical Student Organizations (CTSOs), where all of the State Officers from each student organization under the New Mexico Career and Technical Leadership Project (CTLP) would come together to learn all the resources and strategies we will use to lead out an incredible year for the members in each CTSO.

After a quick drive Northeast to Portales, we arrived at the university where our training was scheduled. Not long after arriving, I found some of my fellow officers, and we helped each other get to our assigned dorm rooms. As I entered my dorm, I freshened up and returned downstairs so we could head over to the training center. We walked in, and the theme of our training this year was all around Hogwarts School of Witchcraft and Wizardry from Harry Potter. From the looks of it, we could tell our training was going to be intense yet, one of the most fun experiences we have ever had while learning new things. As each day went on, not only did we learn many new things, but we were also able to build strong friendships with our team-mates along with State Officers from other CTSOs, which genuinely helped this experience to be even better. One evening during the training, we had to resolve some con-flict between a group of people with a lot of tension, which I was partially a part of. A group of Officers from different CTSOs went into a room with one of our trainers to dis-cuss everything. It was a ton of deep conversation, as ev-eryone was very transparent. Not only did that discussion help us resolve the initial conflict we were experiencing, but it truly brought us closer, and I was thankful for it. During one of our final team times another evening, the New Mexico BPA State Officers gathered in a cool conference room with yarn strung all around the furniture like a maze. Once the coaches handed us our end of the yarn, the goal was to follow the path to find the paper at the end, which would have the title we would serve for our term in office. After some time spent with my teammates, scavenging around the conference room to get to the end of our yarn, we finally made it. Once I opened the paper, it said that I would serve as the 2017-2018 Middle School Representative. This news was exciting because now, I get to help middle schoolers become a part of our organization. I wished this was an opportunity for me to start while in middle school. As we wrapped up the next training day, it was a little sad that we would have to leave each other soon. Yet, it was a celebration moment as we had just completed our very first training as State Officers.

The next thing to prepare for was our Fall Leadership Rallies, where the State Officers would train all of the Chapter Officers from each school across the state in each respective organization. It was also time to get back to school for my junior year. At this point in my education, I was performing well. There were still different areas where I would struggle. It usually came down to procrastination as I felt the greater need to continue breaking out of how my teachers tried to help me learn and find a way to educate myself using my preferred learning style. One thing I did know was that my grades were an even higher priority now because my true passion was serving on the State Officer Team. To do that, you need to uphold a certain Grade Point Average (GPA). As soon as we passed the first few weeks of the new school year, things were going smoothly again. I would always be at the school after regular hours as my extra time consisted of hosting BPA Chapter Meetings as the Chapter President or helping to host some sort of fundraiser, including the concession stand to raise the funds we needed to attend our State and National Leadership Conferences.

The time for our fall conferences came up quickly, and I felt good about my part of the script we would be presenting during the opening and closing sessions of the event. It was another drive up to Albuquerque, and I was nervously excited about this event. This conference would now be the second time I would speak on stage, but it would be the first time in front of students from all the other CTSOs. We did a few rehearsals before the event started, and I became comfortable with the parts that I had memorized. Reading the script was one of my biggest challenges as a State Officer, being that no matter how big the text printed on the sheet that was up on the podium, it would still be hard for me to read, which is why I often resorted to memorizing my scripts as much as possible. Needless to say, I did a pretty good job of carrying a strong stage presence. Thinking back, I am only getting better each time I am up on the stage, as expected, because practice makes professional, not perfect. There were so many fantastic adventures as an officer within the next few months, along with other awesome things such as school and the thought of attending college within the next two years. One excellent part was going to the Sadie Hawkins dance with an extremely good friend of mine. She and I had so much fun with all the laughs during our pictures at the local photo ops and a delicious dinner, followed by a great dance.

Around this same time of the year, there was one night when I was just about to dose off to sleep, and I noticed my phone would not stop making noise. I grabbed my glasses, zoomed in on my screen, and saw that there were reports of an active shooter in Las Vegas, NV. My heart sank, and right as it did, I could hear my dad's phone ringing. It was my sister calling to tell him that there was a shooter at the concert she was at with a few of her friends. Multiple people were shot, and many of them were dead. My sister said she had run to seek cover, and all her friends lost one another. At this point, she had run with some other concertgoers into what seemed to be an airport hangar while hiding behind vehicles and other shielding objects to cover themselves on the way there. I could only imagine how scary this situation was for everyone there, seeing this happen right before their eyes, especially with the lack of awareness as to where the shooter was or where what sounded like multiple shooters to them were shooting from. I stayed up all night looking at various reports and live news networks to get the latest on whether they found the shooter or shooters in the case there were multiple, hoping that with what I discovered there, I could update my sister on where not to go. After countless hours, which likely felt like days to those affected, my sister and her friends were thankfully able to reconnect with no physical injuries. However, there were still people many hours into the next day whose bodies were still lying in the proximity of the concert who sadly lost their lives as a result of some-one else's lack of humanity, which brought horror to thou-sands of lives who were all trying to enjoy an outstanding concert. Our hearts go out to all the families who lost their loved ones and to those who will forever remember this gruesome day that played out right in front of their eyes. I am so grateful that my sister and her friends did not have to experience physical harm during this tragedy. Blessed is an understatement. This incident is another case of many that caused me to question what I could do to help make a change to keep people safe.

As we quickly rolled into the Spring, it was time to be-gin preparing for CTSO Day at the Roundhouse and the Regional and State Leadership Conferences. The cool thing was, now that I am a State Officer, I get to work alongside my team to lead out the CTSO Day at the Roundhouse as well as our State Leadership Conference. This capacity did mean more time on stage. Yet, I was starting to get the hang of it as I began formulating my own process to overcome the barriers that prevented me from reading a script while behind the podium. With CTSO Day at the Roundhouse, we, as State Officers, would invite student leaders from all schools and all organizations across the state to meet in the State Capitol Building, also known as the Roundhouse, in Santa Fe, NM. While at this event, we spoke to our senators and representatives, advocating for state funding to support the amazing things we were able to do in each of our respective organizations. Not to mention getting recognized on the Senate floor. This experience was one of my favorite events of the year. By this point in my journey, I had undoubtedly discovered a passion for student organizations. When it came time for our regional competition, I was excited to have placed in the Top 3, allowing me to advance to state in Prepared Speech. Then came the time to get ready for our State Leadership Conference. As State Officers, we had the opportunity to not only speak at every session but also host our own leadership workshop. I also recognize that I highly valued my first year of service as a State Officer so much that it was essential to run again for the opportunity of re-election to another term in office. This year's theme of my campaign was "No Limits," with the American Flag to showcase the statewide impact we could make to be recognized more nationally as a state that was defining the new standard.

Once we were back at the location for the state conference, it was a similar process to what I did last year, such as taking my things up to the room, freshening up, and getting to work. This time around, I had a different set of responsibilities since I am now part of hosting the conference alongside my fellow State Officers on top of showcasing the things my team and I were able to accomplish throughout our term in office for the chance to get re-elected and expand further on the renowned initiatives that were already in the works. My competitive event came up quicker than expected. I had already memorized a large portion of my scripts for the sessions we were leading as State Officers. Yet, I didn't feel comfortable with the 5-7 minute speech I had to present for my Prepared Speech competition. I was a nervous wreck because the time spent practicing for this competitive event didn't seem like enough. All I knew was that it was time to go into the competition room and do my absolute best for the judges, as there was no going back now. Once I exited the room, it felt like a boulder was lifted off my chest. Now, all I had to focus on was networking with all the student leaders from all across the state and hosting an exceptional workshop with my team. The workshop went so well, and now we anticipate the awards session, anxious to find out who placed in their competitions and which of us candidates will be elected to serve in the upcoming State Officer term.

Immediately as the doors opened, we turned up the music and led the members to get excited about the conference's final session. It was such a fun experience to literally be living in the moment. Our session started, and the State Officers began speaking our parts of the script to open up the session. It quickly came time to play the farewell speeches we recorded on one of our first days at the conference. The farewells were an emotional time as I grew genuinely close to my teammates, and now this was our final time together as State Officers. Once the inspirational farewells wrapped, we got into the announcement of competition placement for awards. The top 10 of every competition were recognized on stage and provided a medal. The top 3 to 5 would be awarded plaques with the opportunity to travel to the National Leadership Conference to compete against top competitors nationwide. I usually competed in the competitions that were announced further towards the end, yet this year, it wasn't a big deal to me as I was able to hand out plaques and medals to winners in all the other competitions, which was a really awesome experience. After about 45 minutes of announcing many winners, the competition results I was anxious about came for Prepared Speech. I heard each of the names of those who are in the top 10, and they were already on the 7th name. I was thankful that my name was announced next as a top 10 competitor. Then, all 10 of us made our way onto the stage. The announcer called 3rd place, then 2nd place, then first place. I wasn't in the top 3. However, it was liberating to know that I had placed in the top 10 because it's apparent I was continuing to overcome my fear of public speaking the more I did it. I could see the potential to become even better by working harder for it every day without question.

When the awards announcements concluded, it was

time to announce who would serve on the 2018-2019 New Mexico BPA State Officer Team. It was exciting to hear my name called, as I would now be serving as the Vice President of Membership throughout the upcoming membership year. As the conference wrapped, it was exciting to reflect and celebrate everyone's accomplishments. Yet, it was a little sad because it was time to say my official goodbyes to my now-former State Officer team. Everything had looked about all cleaned and packed up to this point. It was time to take the three-hour drive back to Roswell, following the pitstop for a Chick-fil-A Spicy Chicken Sandwich with Colby Jack Cheese and Mayo. I can't forget to mention the Large, Sweet Tea.

Once we arrived home and got comfy in bed, it was essential to set my alarm so I could wake up for school the next couple of days. My thoughts were wild that night, thinking about the fact that I had just completed a year in office where I initially spoke for the first time on stage ever in order to get elected, followed by at least 10 more speeches presented in front of a crowd while placing top 10 in the state for Prepared Speech and being re-elected to serve my 2nd term in office. At that point, I also started thinking about the fact that there were only a few months left of Junior year, and I was going to be a Senior the following school year. At some point after that, my brain quickly drifted into a deep sleep until my alarm nearly blew my ears out 8 hours later to wake up for school. For those next few months, it was indeed a repetition of school and BPA activities for both my school, where I was the Chapter President, and the state, where I was just elected as the Vice President of Membership, followed by some decent sleep after the ACT college entrance exam prepping. There wasn't much sleep in the schedule either, especially since this was a time that I began to start taking dual-credit courses out at the college down south of town, which consisted of an Intro to Psychology and Intro to Sociology course. Summer came around lightning fast again, maybe even quicker than last summer. I was excited yet again as I would return to my second State Officer training with New Mexico CTLP. I had also just received the nomination from my school to attend the New Mexico Boys' State event that is hosted every summer by the American Legion, where young men between their Junior and Senior years of high school attend and run for offices at the local, county, state, and some national positions, which replicate the positions of elected government officials so that we can learn all about the processes of what it takes to get elated into those roles and see what each role looks like after being elected. My first summer event was Boys' State, with my State Officer training being the week right after.

Once I arrived at Boys' State, I had to stop by the front desk to pick up my t-shirts and my nametag with the picture they had just taken of me and get sorted into 1 of 4 cities where I got assigned to Armijo. We then went into a room in our city to meet our other brothers from the city. During this first huddle, I randomly started getting nosebleeds all of a sudden because of the dry heat from the weather. Once we met our city brothers, we did our first election to see who was going to serve in each office for the city. I was elected to serve as Armijo's Chaplain, which I found fitting as I was already praying with some of the other guys in my city. We then went into county elections, where two cities would combine to make the county and go through the same process of electing people into county positions. I decided not to run for a county position because I wanted to go all in and run for a state-level office. Once we wrapped up with the county elections, we finished the day with some fascinating activities and a great dinner from the campus cafeteria before heading back to the dorm. It was a little weird at first going to the dorm because this was only my second experience with a roommate, yet the guy I was rooming with was awesome, and it never failed that we would have some extremely great conversations. The next day came, and we woke up bright and early to shower as quickly as possible and head out to the flag pole for the morning routine before breakfast. It was so cool to experience a simulation of how this process is conducted in the military and participate in various drills that helped us become stronger as a team. Once thing to note here was the meal times as I had to remove my top retainer in order to each and the retainer had a fake tooth of mine that my orthodotist had inserted as that was the tooth that had been partially shot out as a result of the shooting and later fully extracted due to infection from the lead pellet that was still lodged inside of it. This was something I had to do every day back at school yet, it wasn't an action I was used to doing anywhere besides school and at home. Anyways, the rest of this day would consist of electing state offices such as State Senators and Representatives. I was up to run for Governor, so I took whatever confidence I had acquired up to this point and went with it. It was quite a process, understandably. Yet, I prepared myself to tackle whatever the world threw at me, ready or not. We had a fictional money currency at Boys' State, so I gathered my money and went to the office to purchase a newspaper advertisement to showcase my candidacy for Governor in the Primary Election. Seeing how it came out in the final print was so cool. One thing that I was still trying to get the hang of was the comfort of conversing with the guys when it came to talking about my candidacy for Governor in the Primary Election. Talk about being an introverted extrovert! It was another day full of great experiences, learning, and leading.

As the night came in, so did the time for Primary Elections. The election process was cool to see, as there was a computer lab we would go into with our login information to submit our ballot. It looked so official, which was awesome. Later, I discovered I hadn't made it past the Primary Election. Regardless, my pride was high because I performed about three more public speaking reps throughout the process and later heard that it was only two votes that prevented me from advancing on to the General Election.

This news was a win in my book. I decided to join in with the guy who did make it through to the General Election because I knew who he was from BPA, and I could learn some great things from him as he was a top-level student leader in our literal state. It turns out he would be the one who got elected as the New Mexico Boys' State Governor. After he was sworn into office, I had the privilege of being appointed by him into the Governor's Cabinet as the Secretary of Public Education, which became a noteworthy position to role play in and see the impact this position has on our state's education system. For a decent portion of the day, we all acted in our respective roles to get the full experience of drafting, vetoing, and passing bills through the legislative body. On the last day, we continued taking many pictures with our brothers, who felt like a literal family after spending a few days with each other and saying our goodbyes. I knew going forward that Boys' State was an experience I would never forget as it helped shape me that much further into the leader I plan on becoming, not necessarily in the government, but in life.

I returned home for a few days to rest and pack to head out for my State Officer training on the same campus where we had Boys' State. I was excited to see the new team I was serving with this year and spend time getting to know each other more in preparation to lead a great year for our members. For this specific training, the theme was all about Disney. It was an awesome experience to connect all the great leadership lessons and tools back to various elements expressed by all our favorite Disney shows and movies. One of my many favorite parts of the training was creating a trail mix with different ingredients by conducting the proper actions of Parliamentary Procedure. The quantity and quality of leadership development encountered over the week of this State Officer training is an experience I can honestly say goes unmatched. One thing I couldn't believe when returning home was that I would soon be entering my Senior year of high school. This point marked a moment in time that seemed so far away to the point where it nearly felt impossible. I hadn't thought about the future for too long because the first day of school was here by the time I knew it. It is always such a fun time to start a new school year, as I was blessed to have a refreshed wardrobe. It almost made me feel like I was becoming a new version of myself each year, even though my clothing often had a pretty similar style. As I entered my senior year, I began to discover that it wasn't my clothes that truly made me feel like a new version of myself. It was all of the things I was experiencing throughout life itself, the good and the bad. All that to say, senior year was off to a pretty great start. I was thankful that some of the things I got involved in at school were now a little more relaxed, although the other parts did seem to become a little more intense. Especially my English class. I have never been the best at school overall. As I've mentioned, I often struggle with the reality of learning according to somebody else's standards and expectations. Don't get me wrong, I LOVE to learn new things, yet it often has to be on my own terms with things that interest me. If provided the space to become educated on topics I love—and topics I don't love so much—with the ability to learn in the ways I learn best, I would become a knowledge powerhouse because I'd be learning with no boundaries of what or how to learn. I later realized that this is why I struggled in school ever since I can remember. Thankfully, I had incredible people to support me in my education, allowing me to move on to the next grade according to schedule and enter the final year of my secondary education. Specifically, in my English class, we had a project where we had to select a topic to do additional research on by reading a book or multiple books from credible sources and drafting a report on the claim we were planning to make while also utilizing the concept of creating an annotated bibliography to help analyze our sources along the way while learning to properly cite sources in MLA format. Wow, I almost ran out of breath trying to share what that project entails. It makes sense because this is going to be one of the most intense projects I have done in my entire academic history. Yet again, if the things I have to learn are not about something I am passionate about or mildly interested in, to say the least, consider it not done. The only way I could get anything done was by hearing the voices of Mrs. Romero and Ms. Grant in my head, cheering me on to get my work done. After a brief thought session where I listed out ideas that I could study, I settled on the concept of analyzing research that has been done so far that shows the impact of implementing spiritual faith into medical care and how the success of medical mysteries differs with and without spiritual faith as a factor in a patient's medical treatment. I found an incredible book titled, "Where God and Medicine Meet" by Neale Donald Walsch and Dr. Brit Cooper. They say to never judge a book by its cover. However, the title alone told me this was the book I needed for my project. Mrs. Romero and Ms. Grant helped hold me accountable for this project, for which I am endlessly thankful. Depending on what part of the book I was on, they would take my print copy of the book over to our library to get it copied onto large 8.5" x 14" or 11" x 17" paper with 18pt to 24pt text so that I could easily read along while highlighting pieces that I believed were noteworthy and later transfer over that content to my annotated bibliography for supporting evidence to my claim. Over the weeks, if not months that it took me to complete this project, I was exhausted yet significantly proud of what I was able to do. I will never forget the support I had throughout that entire project, though. My grade on that assignment was undoubtedly a testament to the work we put into the project every and every day. I couldn't have been more proud, and it only set me up with the mindset that if I could do something like that, I should take the advice of my many favorite authors and begin writing my own books.

Everything was moving so quickly, and it was simultaneously standing completely still. I have been studying for the ACT exam for quite a long time. It was critical to dive into that since it was already a year past the optimal time for me to take this exam. One of my mentors, Ms. Grant, who has helped carry me through high school up to this point, helped me prepare to take the ACT. When it came time to test, I spent my extended amount of allotted testing time very seriously as I had to ensure I was not overcomplicating my answer to each question, which continues to be a pretty common problem of mine. After completing the exam, all the contents were submitted for grading, followed by the waiting period to see my scores.

After a time that felt like forever, I could finally log in to the portal and view my ACT scores. This moment was an exciting yet anxious time as I was worried I would have to retake this exam multiple times in order to have a legitimate score to get into any college. Little did I know, I scored a 30 composite, which, at the time, I thought I horrifically bombed the exam, scoring 30 out of 100 points. This assumption was thankfully not the case because this score meant I had a very high score, allowing me the eligibility to apply for the honors programs at the few colleges I had been looking at applying to. College applications were being completed and submitted immediately following this news. It wasn't until a week later that I received an acceptance letter from a college I had endlessly been praying to get into, Lubbock Christian University (LCU). After receiving this acceptance letter, I knew this was the place that I needed to be as I began my collegiate education. Since the shooting happened about 5 years back, I sensed a calling to serve in the medical field, specifically to become a Pediatric Trauma Surgeon. With that, my plan while attending LCU was to attain my Bachelor of Science in Biochemistry. This degree would then be followed by attending my four years of medical school at the Texas Tech University Health Sciences Center School of Medicine, followed by any residencies and fellowships that came about to become an attending physician in the Pediatric Intensive Care Unit. While completing the remainder of my senior year, I continued researching other medical school options to ensure I would also pursue this portion of my education at a place I felt was most right for me. Ivy League institutions were very much part of my thought process at this period of time as I felt inclined to go big.

Before I knew it, our few breaks were already past, and graduation day was right around the corner. I had decided to go in and talk to the Principal, Mr. Lovett, at the school with an eager hope that he would allow me to speak at our graduation ceremony. I had pondered about this for a while and knew that it was something I had to do. It wasn't anything about me getting to speak in front of my fellow graduates and all the supporting attendees in the stands. It was nothing close to that. This pursuit was coming from a place where I knew many of the people I was graduating with were in the gym with me on the day of the shooting five years ago. They saw everything that happened on that tragic day, which is a picture many of them still carry in their minds to this day, causing who knows what types of challenges in their lives. I wanted to share a message, letting them know that despite all of these things we struggled with in the public eye and all the other things in the deepest, darkest corners of the private worlds in our minds, we were still able to make it through the craziness of high school and come out on top as the graduating Class of 2019.

All throughout high school, I experienced an extensive period of social isolation. I wouldn't talk to many people, even the friends I spent a lot of time with back in middle school. Interestingly, this situation was usually because I am completely blind in one eye with limited vision to see anyone's facial characteristics without being right up in their face. I would walk in the hallways and be able to see well enough to dodge the bodies that filled them. If people came up to me and I didn't already know their voice by heart, I would have no clue as to who I was talking to. The cool thing was that I had a few friends who knew this about me, and every time they would walk up, they said, "Hey Nathaniel! It's [Their Name]," and we would continue with a great conversation. Looking back, I was hoping that people never thought I was ignoring them or being rude as that was never any intention of mine yet, definitely something I couldn't control. All that to say, I knew my full intention with what I planned to say in the message during the graduation ceremony. I decided that the concept would connect back to the natural elements of life. Each element symbolizes the ups and downs that we have experienced in the past, along with all of those that we will unexpectedly experience in the future. By understanding that life is a constant flow of the current, we wouldn't be able to decide what happens to us, yet we can decide how we are going to react to it. I took a long while to think and pray through each portion of this message before sending Mr. Lovett my final draft. Once approved, I started studying and practicing the script I had written. I quickly realized that I didn't need to study the script word for word because it was entirely written from the heart. What I needed to do even more was share this message from the heart without allowing my self-doubt to sneak back in, preventing the message from sticking with my fellow graduates. Once I had my mind and heart aligned on the message I was going to share, it was time to take all of my graduation announcements to the post office.

As soon as graduation day came, I decided to relax the majority of the day, giving me time to truly reflect on all the highs and all the lows throughout my time in high school and understand that I had overcome a lot of challenges in order to accomplish the achievements I have so far. It was also a time when I looked at all the people who surrounded me during every moment, ensuring that no matter how far I fell, there was always someone there to pull me out of the pits I had fallen into at different times in my life. Just when I began to wrap up my reflection session, the alarm on my phone came blaring through my Bluetooth speaker, which I had forgotten my phone was connected to, telling me it was time to start getting dressed for the graduation ceremony. I took another shower to ensure I was nice and clean before putting on my dress shirt and slacks, as it was clearly time to get down to business. I placed my cap and gown in the truck and headed to the Wool Bowl with my parents. As I hopped off the truck, the staff directed me to where I needed to go, and I was able to meet up with Mr. Lovett before the ceremony. After having some memorable conversations with multiple people, the music began playing, and we started making our way down the football field toward our seats. It was a moment where I was in awe of what was in front of me. It was a stadium filled with people who helped us graduates get to this very moment. I felt all the positive emotions knowing my family, friends, and staff who supported me along the way were there to witness me walk across the stage and flip the tassel.

Once I found my seat, we began the commencement ceremony. Soon after, Mr. Lovett went up to welcome me to the stage. It was a moment where my nerves went through the roof, yet it wasn't because I was nervous about speaking in front of people. It was because I wanted to ensure I presented this message in a way that made the positive impact I intended it to make. Once I quickly gathered myself and knew what I needed to do, I proudly walked up onto the stage. As I approached the mic, the wind was blowing pretty hard, making everyone's graduation swag fly around. It was quite ironic as this wind was exactly what I needed. This component was so on theme with my message as it connected to the elements. The first few sentences came out while my mind began to think. Once I noticed myself doing too much thinking, I simply let the words from my heart flow. Once I finished, the crowd entered into a brief moment of silence, followed by a standing ovation from everyone in the stadium. As soon as I heard the cheers, I knew that my message made the impact I hoped it would make for all who heard it.

The commencement continued with the many notable names called to the stage, each followed by many celebratory cheers. I went up to the side of the stage with my row of fellow graduates and continued approaching the stage as it got closer to the time to walk the stage. As I reached the top of the stairs, one of my biggest supporters who helped get me through high school, Ms. Grant, was up on the stage. As we heard "Nathaniel Ryan Tavarez," she would be the one to hand me my diploma. It was undoubtedly a moment I will remember forever, with a great photo that captures it all. Not long after, the graduation ceremony adjourned, the sky filled with fireworks and graduation caps, and the crowds came down to the field, giving countless celebratory hugs. This moment became a time for me when time was nearly standing still, and we were literally living in slow motion. High school was now a thing of the past, with a future of many unknowns ahead. However, I know I am prepared for whatever life throws at me next, even if I don't feel ready. After an exhilarating day of celebration, I made my way home for a good night's sleep.

CHAPTER SEVEN
FAILING FORWARD

*"It's not how far you fall, but how
high you bounce that counts."*
– Zig Ziglar

This summer will be full of exciting yet very stressful times. I was ecstatic to return to the New Mexico Boys' State Session as a Junior Counselor, followed by
the New Mexico CTLP State Officer Training as a Trainer.
The stressful part came into play when I began thinking
that I would be moving to a different state within the next
month or two, starting college as a Pre-Medical Student,
majoring in Biochemistry, not to mention the LCU Honors College on top of that. Thankfully, the events I plan
to attend this summer are not the first of that style, which
helped ease some of my nerves. I decided to use my packing for Boys' State as a practice session for the packing I
have to do for college. I packed a few pairs of jeans, jack-
ets, and comfy clothes to sleep in. My giant fuzzy blanket
with a memory foam cooling pillow was next in my bag.
Shirts were unnecessary as the staff provides shirts when

we arrive on-site for Boy's State.

On the drive up to Portales, we stopped at "the burrito" to get the usual meal. It was surreal once we arrived on campus, as my experience here last year was unforgettable, both in the good and the not-so-good ways. Being back as a Junior Counselor was remarkable because it is now my turn to educate these young men who would be the next generation of leaders in our country. I made it to my dorm room and placed my bags down, followed by a quick refresh and change to my Boys' State fit. Then, it was time to head down the hall to meet with my city before we jumped into city elections. As I entered the room, I immediately connected with these guys, as they were now looking up to me as their guide. Someone they aspire to learn from, meaning I would now be stepping into the beginning elements of who I want to become. No matter what I do in the future, my goal is to be a figure for people, showing them that nothing is impossible.

That said, I gave a quick spiel on who I am and what they would learn during our time together. The lecture followed by city elections soon followed. The election was a breeze, so we transitioned to operations of the city government with everyone in their respective elected and appointed roles. After a few hours of city operations, we joined in with another city to begin the procedures of county elections. Similar to what happened in our city, we did a lecture on what positions are open at the county level along with the ways of operation followed by the election and installment into office. Those elected officials acted according to their appropriate duties in alignment with their roles and so on. Now, it was time for the State Legislative procedures. Collectively, all four cities that comprise two counties met in a joint session to conduct the election and appointment of Senators, Representatives, Lieutenant Governor, and Governor, along with the Governor's Cabinet. There was quite an extensive campaigning process as all candidates were vetted by their constituents before entering the Primary Election.

One of the other excellent segments of Boys' State is the talent show we had amidst the educational content, where these boys would showcase various talent-related elements of what they could do outside of any form of government-like environment. After hearing the primary election results, we shifted to all preparations for the General Election, where we discovered which boys had made it to serve as part of the State Legislative body. The pre-election process included the Gubernatorial Debate by the two different teams, each made up of a Lieutenant Governor Candidate and a Governor Candidate. As soon as the debate started, things were already a bit heated, as we often see in most debates amongst candidates of opposition. The time swept by as though we were there for just a few minutes, yet the discussion consisted of educational insight and an elegant dinner, during which we had the pleasure of connecting with the Dean of Students from the University. Soon after, it was time for all the boys to place their votes, concluding the final election of this year's Boys' State session. The staff announced the election results, and we directed all the boys to begin the proceedings in their respective chambers. The Governor's Cabinet was quickly appointed to start up the functionalities for all legislative bills that came across the desk. The legislative session came and went as the rest of this Boys' State session did, which is common every year because, throughout this learning time, every boy makes the greatest of connections with fellow peers, which turn into lifelong friendships. By the end of every session, each boy seems to become more of a man while meeting people who you feel like you've known your entire life. The experience is unmatched. If future responsibilities allow, I will make it a point to return every year to provide each boy with an even better experience than my amazing one.

As it was time to wind down and pack up, the counselors I had the year I first attended as a participant asked me to share my story with our city, and it was so. While telling my story to audiences like this and those before and after, I was beginning to see how much of an impact my story was making. To me, my story happened, and soon after, many people "forgot" about it, or so it seemed. In reality, despite the incident occurring an X amount of years ago, my story never lost its power to positively impact anyone who heard it. It was incredible to see all of these boys in complete silence—which is quite abnormal for most guys their age or any age for that matter—while some were even brought to tears of inspiration and joy when seeing who I am regardless of the tragedy I experienced. We all had a long night's rest with a great breakfast soon after. It was then time to say goodbye to another round of our new best friends and return to our regular summer lives.

When I returned home, it was time to get packed up for the next adventure back to the campus for the New Mexico CTLP State Officer Training. This training is the exact one I've attended as a State Officer in previous years. However, I am now preparing to train these newly-elected leaders on Parliamentary Procedure in alignment with Robert's Rules of Order to help each CTSO's State Executive Council properly conduct business during their virtual meetings and in-person sessions at their conferences. This event was another one that felt surreal as my emotions were running high, thinking that childhood was close to ending and adulthood was rapidly approaching. It was an exhilarating time with a bit of anxiety in the midst.

Once I snapped back to reality, it was time to create another unforgettable experience and learning opportunity for this next generation of leaders. Alongside the wonderful people who taught me much of what I know, I had the chance to pass on the legacy to the next generation of student leaders. There were many moments of collectively teaching and learning now that I am on the other side of the table, along with networking, which led to even more long-lasting friendships. As we concluded this event, my thoughts continuously shifted around the fact that in just a few weeks, I would be physically on my own as a whole adult, yet thankful that my family is always one call away. In the case that I ever have to call and ask them to pick me up from college and take me back home, they would drop whatever they are doing and be there as quickly as possible to get me out of there and back home where I felt safe. This area of my life is one of the countless places where I am abundantly thankful and blessed to have parents and siblings who support me in a multitude of ways.

Speaking of feeling safe, it's unbelievable to think of what our world is becoming because no matter where you go, it's challenging to feel secure. After experiencing the incident I was injured in back in 2014, it seems like things are only getting worse across the nation. Every time I look at my phone, there is some new report of gun violence in schools, churches, concerts, or shopping centers of some sort. As my brain began to think of this, I knew that going into this next chapter of my life, I still had many questions from my past lingering, which felt like they were stunting me from moving forward and taking on the new journeys that lie ahead. That's when I decided to call one of my most favorite people, Ms. Marie, to ask if there was any way I could meet with the shooter and ask him some questions before I moved to college in a few weeks. She made a few phone calls herself, and it wasn't until two weeks later that my mom, my sister, and I were driving up north to the facility where Callum was serving his sentence. The entire day, my emotions filled with stress and anxiety, yet I knew

I had to do this in order to allow myself to move on. As soon as we walked in the door, we were welcomed by the exceptional staff and taken back into the conference room. The nice lady notified me that the shooter would come in, and I was free to ask any questions I would like.

After a few minutes, the officer brought him in, and he was seated right across the table from me. I looked down at my lap in complete silence, contemplating what I was going to ask first since the boy who nearly ended my life was sitting two feet in front of me at this very moment. After what felt like an hour of horrific silence, my prayer led me to gain the courage and finally ask, "Why did you do it?". A brief moment passed, and he replied that he was, in fact, bullied, which led to his actions. The answer was no surprise to me as this was the true and proven statement during the court hearing back in July of 2014. The next thought that came to my mind was asking him if the person's name, which he stated in his journal to be the bully, was actually the person he was targeting. He confirmed with a yes. At this point, even though I knew myself or nobody else aside from that bully and the shooter were at legitimate primary fault for this horrific motive that Callum acted upon, leading to me almost losing my life, I was now curious as to what the shooter planned to do when he was released from state custody in a few years being that he is now 18 and is scheduled for release at the age of 21. His reply was quite surprising but, at the same time, not unexpected whatsoever. It was surprising because Callum envisioned his plan for the future with a positive outlook. However, the approach of this reply didn't seem uncommon as this positive person talking to me now is the person I knew before the incident.

His aspirations were quite impressive, and I had the idea that if our paths ever crossed again—and he and I collectively were comfortable moving forward with a mission—we could join forces for some time and speak out about what we can change in communities all across America to prevent future cases of gun violence. I failed to verbalize this at that moment, so this was a new thing on my mind following this visit. Yet, I know it is something I will address in the near future. Following this nerve-racking visit, it was time to head back home and finish the crazy amount of packing I had imagined necessary to have everything I possibly needed when moving into my dorm.

The morning of moving day, I woke up excessively early. I had to speed through everything I was doing because most of my stuff had yet to be packed, and my dad had suggested for weeks to pack early. All these weeks, I was in a place of mixed emotions where I was excited to be entering into a stage of so many beginnings while, at the same time, feeling afraid of leaving home and departing from all that I knew and all that I was comfortable with. Despite any negative thoughts or hard feelings that attempted to hold me back, I knew I was entering into a season of yeses where nothing could hold me back but me, myself, and I. Especially when it came to becoming comfortable with being uncomfortable. As soon as I could gather myself and everything I would be taking to college, we made one last stop at "the burrito" and hit the road to Lubbock, Texas. A nap felt very necessary after the insane early morning that we had already had.

Not long after closing my eyes, I opened them, and we were already pulling into the parking lot of my dorm. As we drove up, you could already see a ton of fellow college students, with a few of their family members and friends moving into the dorm rooms. I had already felt out of place because most of the students brought a backpack with a luggage case or two, and I'm over here with a small trailer bringing all the things that I love, which would help me to make the dorm room feel like home. It wasn't bad, though, because as soon as we pulled into a parking spot, grabbed my room key, and unloaded everything into my new room, I was able to meet my roommate, and he was pretty cool. The hardest part about that day was that it was the first time I would ever be over a hundred miles away from my parents for any longer than a couple of days.

As I mentioned earlier, the best part about my family is that a phone call was all it would take for them to turn around to come back for me and take me back to the comfortable place I called home. I do have to say that in the first few weeks, there were a couple of times that I had the idea of calling them to come and get me for the weekend. Yet, if I started giving in now, I would never achieve the great things I envisioned nor become the person I dreamed of becoming if I began to limit myself in any way. The entire first half of my first semester was a full period of transition with many feelings of homesickness as I was literally sick for the entire first month. No over-the-counter medications were on my side, so doctor's visits were constant.

I entered college as a Biochemistry Major and Pre-Medical Student in the Honors College. This path meant many classes were now a thing by choice, and I had enrolled in 18 credit hours this Fall Semester. My mind told me since I was in 8 classes every year in high school, 6 to 7 college courses a semester would be a breeze. One of the things that I also struggled to say no to is the opportunity to get involved on campus since I convinced myself of being in this season of yeses. That meant running for Student Senate, which I was appointed into, serving briefly on the Honors Student Advisory Board, participating in the pre-health club, and seeing what some social clubs had to offer during Rush Week. Being that I was now in the same location as the hospital where the doctors helped save my life back in 2014, I decided I would also jump in there to kick off my internship and volunteer opportunities, allowing me to expand my portfolio, which would be huge when it came to my medical school application.

I also took it upon myself to start a Facebook Live series called "Leadership Lounge," where I shared content on leadership topics to help people become better leaders. This series is where I began to learn about practicing what you preach. It wasn't but a month into the semester when

I was already overwhelmed and burnt out. At one point, we were assigned a twelve-page research paper on a topic of our choosing. When doing schoolwork, I was always up for the challenge. However, I would enter into a state of paralysis because I always wanted my work to be extraordinarily perfect, which led to procrastination where I would plan how to do it flawlessly yet not initiate the project until a day or two before the due date and the finished product was not my best as I had intended. Regardless, I ended up choosing a topic that meant a lot to me, and this led to many weeks of working on this particular research project on the rise of gun violence in schools, churches, concerts, and shopping centers across America, followed by strategies that can we can utilize to reverse the trending lines, lowering and one-day ending gun violence once and for all. This assignment had to have been the hardest I had ever worked on a school project, likely because this is a topic I am passionate about, as this is one of the main parameters I need met to enjoy the learning process.

Out of that entire first semester, this was the one and only thing I am proud of. This assignment led me to brainstorm many other great things I imagined could be possible within the school safety and mental wellness space, moving forward with further research outside the assignment. Soon after, the number of late nights and early mornings caught up to me at such a rapid pace to the point where I would take the "rest days" that I chose for myself yet, keeping track to make sure I didn't miss too many classes and fall significantly behind on my coursework. Yet again, I overestimated, but this time on what I could hit pause on and did fall behind to the point of no return. My first semester of college was academically the worst I had ever done in any of my education since I even knew what school was. I tended to constantly beat myself up about this because the idea of becoming a Pediatric Trauma Surgeon was very real to me. I knew I could achieve this if it were something I put my mind to.

Up to this point, I had already made some pretty great friends. However, I made sure to keep my social circle pretty tight because, based on past experiences, the more "friends" you have, the more likely you are to be stabbed in the back multiple times and nearly left for dead. I was also beginning to see the fact that in the world we live in, everyone must fend for themselves. One person could be your best friend, and the moment you turn around, they are stealing from you. This situation is one I have experienced way too many times. Similarly, your coworkers could be so nice that you believe you are on the same team. Yet, the second something goes wrong that was equally or solely their fault, you will be the first person they blame to ensure they keep their job with no care about how it may negatively affect you.

All that to say, the semester was over much quicker than it seemed. I had learned a ton about life over the past five months, yet I didn't feel like I learned much from school itself as I had started to bury most anything related to school deep down due to my underperformance that I was ashamed of. One of the biggest highlights of what I learned had to be the fact of learning to say no, as every no you say could lead to more yeses for things that will be more effective and beneficial for you. My favorite part was the fact that Christmas Break was here, and now was the time to go back home and spend time with my family for more than just a few days.

On Christmas day, it was such a great feeling to have all of my family back together in one room, celebrating the birth of Jesus while enjoying the delicious food my dad always made for the holiday season. Over the break, I did some self-evaluation to see where I underperformed this past semester and what I can do moving forward as I return in the Spring. I knew that all these extracurricular things I tried to take on would no longer be a thing and not by choice. I was learning how to say no, but it was a big transition for me, being that I continuously said yes to everyone and everything over all these years. My grades were horrific, and it was time to buckle down. At this point, I need to perform so well if I want even the slightest chance of getting into medical school. By the time I reflected on where all my time went in the Fall and made a plan for improvement in the Spring, it was already time to head back to campus.

This particular semester, I had the same dorm room all to myself. This semester was my opportunity to not only get back on track but to fully dive into the things that would help me become a stronger candidate for medical school. I enrolled in a decent majority of the same classes that I had in the Fall because I wanted to get to the point where I could raise my GPA, which is one of the many factors in having a competitive application. It was also a great idea to begin logging my volunteer and internship hours, so I went directly to the hospital where my life was saved and applied for these opportunities in the pediatrics unit. At the start of the semester, I had a good hold on things, especially while utilizing many of the productivity tools and strategies I had learned over Christmas Break.

The semester was yet another that had seemed to fly by while simultaneously standing still. I was constantly going to all of my classes, getting a decent majority of my chapel credits, and logging volunteer hours at the hospital as a Child Life Specialist. In the evenings, I would attend various meetings or events for Student Senate and any campus events that could help me expand the growth of my Christian faith. I finally realized this semester that it wasn't bad to ask for help, such as utilizing the campus resources, including tutoring services alongside the student mentoring program.

As I began operating more effectively in managing all of these pieces, I saw improvement in multiple areas of my life, including academics. Although my grades were still not where I had intended, I knew that it was time to begin celebrating the small wins and slow down on stressing myself out around the clock. Mid-semester, I received an email from our campus communications that we would be shifting to a virtual learning environment since the United States officially declared a national emergency due to the pandemic. I initially thought this semester would finish smoothly, but that was not the case.

I shifted back and forth from my parent's house in Roswell to my sister's house in Lubbock for the remainder of the semester. Otherwise, returning home as instructed. From my perspective, I had already been performing in this productivity loop that I believed to be effective because it worked for me. Now, I had to revise all my operations to a virtual world. This approach came to me as a whole new life, as I'm sure it did for many others. By the time the semester ended, it felt like I was back at square one, as my grades had fallen again. I had to remind myself about celebrating the small wins while reflecting on my life, so this small win was the fact that I had just finished my first full year of college, and I was still functioning somehow. I wasn't a fan that we had to understandably wear face masks everywhere we went to protect ourselves and those around us, mainly because my glasses constantly fogged up. What hurt my heart was the fact that thousands of people were dying from this insane illness called Coronavirus, also referred to as COVID-19. Despite the crazy times we were now in, one thing that came to my attention for the summer was the thought that I could get a job and start making some money for myself.

Since I now live in Lubbock, I first submitted a job

application at the store of my favorite athletic wear brand. Not long after submitting my application and completing the interview process, I got hired as a Seasonal Sales Associate. I kicked off my first week of the job in a hands-on training, learning the ins and outs of operating the storefront. The following week, my fellow new hires and I were jumping straight into the various areas we were assigned to for each shift, ranging from working the sales floor, the back of the house where many other products were stored, the registers, or handling the front door where we had to give customers who were entering a facemask with hand sanitizer while also keeping track of how many customers were in the store to maintain social distancing to the best of our ability.

The first couple of weeks on the job were great. When things started to get challenging for me was after a conversation I had with one of the managers about why I was only being out on the sales floor a shift here and there, never getting to work the register, and most often being the primary person to handle the door during most of my shifts. This manager's excuse was that since I have low vision, he didn't believe I could operate the register or perform on the sales floor. After taking a breath and attempting to understand his perspective, I shared with him that I am willing to come in early before my shifts or stay after my shifts entirely unpaid to execute my own training on the registers outside of business hours. He immediately denied my request and said I was better off managing the door and occasionally working on the sales floor if he felt it was possible. That operational structure was precisely how he laid out my shifts in the following weeks. It had become quite irritating as time went on. Especially when I would be criticized by that same manager while working the sales floor because he allegedly observed that I was refolding shirts "too slowly" despite there being no customers in the store and the other employees on shift standing around gossiping with each other, including that same manager. Being talked to in that type of way is not something I, nor anyone else, is a fan of, although my perception of the bigger picture is that we are all on the clock, getting paid for the work put in by the hour, which means I was there to do my job, committed to doing every task to the best of my ability. My effort was not for the manager's benefit either, but for my own benefit to know that I did my job at my absolute best, no matter the task.

A few more weeks passed, and we were already getting close to the holiday season. That manager printed our schedules roughly two or three weeks in advance, and I saw that I was working on Halloween. This particular holiday is one that I didn't necessarily mind missing. Yet, seeing that he scheduled me to work on that same day, it prompted me to request time off for Thanksgiving and Christmas, as these are two holidays I refuse to miss being with my family. While making the verbal request to my manager, I was cut off mid-sentence and told that nobody else could take off for the holidays as the maximum amount of staff was already on vacation during that time. At this point, I felt fed up for a while with the way that many of my coworkers and I got treated and talked to, so I put in my two weeks' notice, and during my very next shift, that manager called me into his office where he notified me that I was relieved of my job duties right then and there. I was thankful for that since I now didn't have to spend another two weeks under the most sickening case of micromanaging I'd ever heard of. The way I explained this particular job experience doesn't do justice, as I kept it light for everyone's sanity. As I reflected on the experience overall, I acknowledged that as my long-term goal, I would not work for someone else moving forward, which brought me into this mental state of becoming an entrepreneur no matter the exact industry I pursue in the future.

At this time, my mind began to ponder, questioning if becoming a Pediatric Trauma Surgeon or any Medical Doctor was right for me. There was a feeling I had for so long that medicine was my calling. Yet, as days, weeks, and another semester went by, I discovered that medicine may not be where my true calling lies, and this is why I am experiencing various situations that lead me to where God has actually called me to serve his divine purpose for my life. Throughout this contemplation sequence, I knew I wanted to help people. However, medicine isn't the only place you can do that. It became clear that I had many ambitions. In fact, I have so many aspirations, which is why I always feel that I am making zero progress no matter how hard I work, always reaching in a multitude of directions.

One thing I do know is since I am at the stage in my life where I still have so much flexibility to change everything in a flash, I needed to continue exploring all of my ambitions to discover where it felt right, no matter the challenges and obstacles that came with it. It wasn't long before I purchased all my equipment and filed my business paperwork to formulate a Limited Liability Company (LLC) called Hustlyn Co., a motivational apparel company with graphics that intended to ignite a shift and keep people in a positive head space so that they too could see success and endless happiness in their life. While spending countless hours on my laptop, I discovered how to build my website and launch an online storefront where people can shop. I created all of the accounts on most social media platforms where I had this giant idea of producing tons of content that could organically market to my target audience, including teens and young adults up to any and every age.

Understanding that this is my first attempt at such a big project with a significant investment, it was clear that this was difficult in many ways as I had committed to learning as I went and managing every imaginative department that I believed needed to be in existence to see success in my new small business. That said, I posted some content on social media here and there, uploaded new designs to my website, and promoted a little for each design, always looking to see how I could continue making my apparel even better. My sales were decent and steady at a few shirts a week. It was great to see how small progress can create more significant results. At the same time as managing this new venture of mine, classes were still a thing. I noticed that even though I was still taking all my classes for a degree in Biochemistry, my overall performance was improving. I was getting much better grades on my assignments, and any exam didn't cause me to feel that sense of nausea in my stomach. Talk about a moment to celebrate.

BPA, the student organization I mentioned before, was still something I decided to be involved in at the post-secondary, collegiate level. With that, the two competitive events I would consecutively choose each year were Entrepreneurship and Prepared Speech. I had settled in on Entrepreneurship for the upcoming membership year and was already on track with my preparation. Time went on, and I conducted a full rotation of managing school, my small business, and my experiences for the medical school application—knowing that wouldn't be a thing anymore— and preparing for competition. Time flew by with all the great things I was doing, and it all kept me busy. I was sad to see thousands of other students from across the States and I had to shift to a virtual National Leadership Conference. However, it was understandable as this is a time when illness cases due to the pandemic were at an all-time high, causing many events across the nation to simply get cancelled as opposed to shifting to a virtual event.

Competition day was already here, and I was more than ready. I had set up my laptop in the corner of my dorm room and patiently waited for the judges to enter my virtual competition room. As soon as they entered, I introduced myself and kicked off my presentation. I had 5-7 minutes to present my business idea with the plan and strategy as to how I was going to launch my product line and market to the respective target audience, finding success in the selected industry. Thankfully, I had prepared to present within this timeframe as I had talked to the point that it felt like hours, yet I still managed to stay within my timeframe. I felt so good after that presentation that I went to our campus coffee shop and grabbed a large caramel frappe, as it felt well deserved.

Later that evening, we had the Grand Achievement Awards Session to discover the top competitors. This session is always long, yet seeing so many students recognized for such an incredible accomplishment is remarkable. Thankfully, it wasn't too long until I saw Entrepreneurship as one of the upcoming competitive events in the queue. The announcer said, "And now, your top competitors in Entrepreneurship Post-Secondary are..." He continued with Fifth Place. My stomach crunched because it was not my name announced. Then came Fourth Place, and my stomach got tighter. Third Place, I began to squeeze my chair. Second place, I'm pretty sure sweat was dripping from my forehead and chin. "And your First Place National Champion is... Nathaniel Tavarez!" I'm almost positive everyone on campus heard me shout because I was excited to have just won this competition. I'm proud to say I am now a national champion! It felt so good to win and see that kind of success. I had to sit back as I was in shock since I was constantly questioning myself and doubting my capabilities. It became apparent that entrepreneurship is part of my calling, at least in this period of my life. In my approach, entrepreneurship consists of building businesses that can help change people's lives. I even decided to take a couple of Summer courses because I felt empowerment flowing through every cell in my body.

After the Spring semeter finished, I went with my gut and took a Summer course which included lessons on optimal nutrition and physical performance. However, I was also in a place where I wasn't happy with my experience at the campus I was on. Not because of anything the campus did or didn't do necessarily. It felt like I was no longer meant to be at that specific place, and my time there had finished. Did I mention that I completely Aced those summer courses, and my GPA was quite exceptional considering my educational past? Oh yeah, that was certainly a thing. Anyway, while I was completing those summer courses at LCU, I submitted my application to the university across the city and soon received notification that I was accepted. It was time for a fresh start, an entirely new chapter, and I took the opportunity while it was right there in front of me.

CHAPTER EIGHT
REVOLUTION IN MOTION

*"We can't become what we need
to be by remaining what we are."*
– Max Depree

At last, it was time to complete my transition to Texas Tech University. Not only did I quickly transition to start up the upcoming Fall semester. Interestingly enough, I also changed my major to General Human Sciences, intending to get my Bachelor's Degree in Nutritional Sciences. I had also moved into an apartment right down the street from campus. This new pursuit had become such a great experience, especially when I decided to start riding the scooters around campus to class, which got me there in about 10 minutes as opposed to the 30-45 minutes it took me to walk to class. Overall, I knew Texas Tech is now where I am meant to be. The lecture halls are massive, with so many great resources for their various programs, on top of the fantastic food options all across campus. I couldn't ask for anything more. My classes were going decently smoothly, except I continually struggled with Biology, funny enough. No matter where I take it, this biology course is one I cannot seem to grasp, and I have so much self-doubt when it comes to understanding the subject.

On the other hand, I did enroll in a stunning extracurricular program called The Leadership Institute (TLI), which gave me a whole new sense of extraordinary leadership qualities to help build me into a stronger changemaker, not to mention the great friends I made during TLI. When it came to my nutritional sciences coursework, my performance is what I would rank as moderately well. One of the days after class, I rode the electric scooter back to my apartment. After walking through the door and setting my things down, I looked at my phone and saw a message from someone on social media. I clicked on the message and saw a lady saying she had seen my story and asked me if I would mind speaking to her church members over a video call. Feeling so honored, I immediately replied, "YES!"

After preparing my talking points to ensure I shared my message in a way that brought the most influential impact, it was time to share. I logged into the video call and had a great introduction from this amazing lady who initially reached out to me. Then, it was time for me to dive in. Over the next twenty-five minutes or so, I shared all of the details about what happened to me on January 14th, 2014, while highlighting how I felt God's presence throughout my entire healing journey from that point onward. As I wrapped up, there was one phrase from my past weighing heavy on my heart, which was, "Medicine can't explain how I'm alive today, but GOD CAN!" Immediately after, there was a brief moment of silence, and then everyone came off mute, clapping and shouting praises to God for all of His goodness. It was truly transformational. Despite my attempt to integrate my entrepreneurial pursuit into the nutrition-based industry, I realized in this experience that a degree in Nutritional Sciences is definitely not for me. My first semester at Tech was already ending, and I had decided that going all in as an entrepreneur in business felt more right than anything else I had ever attempted. When I had my meeting with the academic advisor, I mentioned that I plan on transitioning to the Rawls College of Business and changing my major to Business Administration with a concentration in Strategic Entrepreneurship and Innovation. Before making that transition, I still had some work to do, yet I am ready to go all in.

The spring semester came fast, and it was time to start on the last courses I needed before transitioning to the business college. One of the other unique opportunities I could jump into was a couple of business competitions at the Texas Tech Innovation Hub at Research Park. These competitions, Red Raider Startup and iLaunch, are intended to allow individuals and teams to pitch various business ideas that they could qualify to advance to the next level of the competition for a chance to get a grant for their startup. At Red Raider Startup, I had a remarkable team where we pitched a mobile application to guide all the extraordinary people within the foster care system to connect for a safe space of relatability and support. The preparation for our pitch was excellent, but sadly, our app prototype did not advance.

That's when I began to prepare my business strictly and pitch for the iLaunch competition, where I would pitch my idea of a Strategic Discipline Monthly Subscription Box, which held various tools and resources subscribers could use as leverage in their journey to becoming the very best version of themselves, unlocking their full potential. This competition was my first time diving so deep into the business realm that after doing my practice run-through with one of the professional mentors at The Innovation Hub, I quickly realized how much I still had to learn about the business industry. Despite not advancing to the next round with this business idea, I was thankful to have uncovered what else I needed to know when it came to business. This discovery fully set out my pursuit of becoming a high-performing entrepreneur, with dreams of creating Fortune 500 companies, not for the money, but for the impact my companies can make on people worldwide.

Shifting back to school, the semester is now over. I performed decently well, yet I know I can do even better. While reflecting on my academic career thus far, I had also jumped into further planning for the future. One of the things that I am passionate about is giving back to the people and the places that have poured so much into me.

With that intention in mind, there is a company that does incredible work with the Career and Technical Student Organizations (CTSOs) I was involved in from the start of high school up to this point now in college. I had reached out to a couple of the teammates of this company a couple of years ago, yet, they were not hiring at the time, and at that point, I was straight out of high school, meaning that I was also relatively inexperienced. I decided to follow up with these same people now that a couple of years had passed. Interestingly enough, I received an email from one of them sharing an opportunity for me to go and facilitate three different workshops at the State Conference for one of the leading CTSOs in California. With complete excitement, I replied with a giant "YES!" The preparation for this conference was in full operation. Part of this prep included the emotional checklist of getting ready to take my first flight alone. Thankfully, the strength of my Christian faith is so enormous that all it took was a few prayers, and I knew this was where I was guided for a much bigger purpose.

Surely enough, I hopped on that flight with my head held high, ready to go "Bring Light to Dark Places," as the company's mission implied. It was at that point that I was officially a Leadership Trainer for the company TEAM-TRI. That is just the beginning of my journey with this transformational company. I couldn't wait to see all the experiences ahead. A few months had passed, and I had shared with my Champion—known to most companies as a manager—that I was interested in becoming a State Officer Coach. Not long after, I had the opportunity to coach not one but two State Officer Teams, each under their own CTSO. The coaching environment was so great that I had the chance to mentor an additional State Officer Team the following year.

My life up to this point had felt so right to the point where I knew this was where I was supposed to be at this moment. The people I am working alongside on top of the people we provide services to, the other people we serve, and the impact we are making are all extraordinary, to say the least. The other part that truly made this experience come together is all the places I've been able to travel across America from North to South and East to West. Seeing the impact we've been able to make within the leadership development space for students and educators across all CTSOs, this is when I was reassured that I needed to take my message and research that I've been conducting for the past six years into the places where we are seeing gun violence across America including schools, churches, and shopping centers to name a few. And it was so that this new endeavor became my central pursuit to innovate holistic safety practices from every perspective possible.

CHAPTER NINE
BUILDING SAFER TOMORROWS

*"Peace cannot be kept by force; it can
only be achieved by understanding."*
– Albert Einstein

Thinking back to some of the projects I worked on in high school, most of the time, the topic I chose to study—when given the option to choose—would always be around Spiritual Faith, Mental Health, and Gun Violence. One of the books I remember reading, followed by a detailed analysis to develop my annotated bibliography in direct alignment for the Senior project, was titled, "Where God and Medicine Meet: A Conversation Between a Doctor and a Spiritual Messenger" by Neale Donald Walsch and Dr. Brit Cooper. While looking for credible sources, this specific book stood out to me because I knew that—as I often say—"Medicine can't explain how I'm alive today, but God can," and the title of this book alone continues to hit a soft spot. While re-reading and re-processing the contents, I could see more light in the context where there is so much alignment with the spiritual and physical worlds regarding the inner workings of healing, especially when you look at all of modern medicine's treatments. It's pretty remarkable what medical professionals can do. However, when you incorporate the approach of medical knowledge and spiritual faith cohesively—such as trusting God as the ultimate guide and healer—into patient care, as Mr. Walsch and Dr. Cooper shared, the success of the overall medical treatment proves to be much more miraculous.

An additional book I discovered shortly after is titled "Becoming Supernatural: How Common People Are Doing the Uncommon" by Dr. Joe Dispenza. This book focuses on the concepts that help connect the mind to the body, showing how our thoughts become our reality and how we can tap into the parts of our minds that can transform our lives into the best they can be. My description of this book is an understatement, as there is so much more Dr. Dispenza has to offer, especially in everything he creates outside of this book. As I moved on to further studies of my own, I noticed that I began to see a pattern of multiple perspectives from a wide selection of people who all had very valid points to consider when addressing the rise of gun violence nationwide. These notable people include students, parents and guardians, educators, and school administrators. These are just some of the directly affected whom I consider the primary stakeholders in my studies. Then, we get into the secondary stakeholders, including but not limited to law enforcement officers, first responders, healthcare workers, mental health professionals, policymakers, and generally anyone else within a community willing to lend a hand in finding a permanent, long-term solution. The diversity amongst each and every one of these individuals across the primary and secondary stakeholder plane is crucial in the collaborative efforts of creating this plan, which I continuously work on developing and revising to fit and expand modern-day systems. Across a selection of conversions I've had with various people so far, I have found that multiple actions should be conducted simultaneously within a school and its community to begin seeing the impact of lowering the number of incidents within a specific period compared to the years prior during that same month, for instance. This particular methodology that I am stating here is what I call the holistic, multi-factor approach. Within this framework are probable solutions ranging in the capacity of mental wellness, threat detection and elimination technology, policies at any level that can impact people's safety while in a physical location, various laws pertaining to weapon safety along with the punishment if people are injured or killed with a weapon, in addition to the constant evolutionary factors that will help to create the best community possible for all of our locals, especially the youth.

Over the many years of research I've conducted so far on these relative topics, it has become clear that there are quite a few organizations with an assortment of outspoken thought leaders who are doing some transformational things to make a change in an effort to end gun violence. In fact, a large majority of the quantitative and qualitative data I've collected across my studies have come from some of these organizations. I am very thankful for all they do in their efforts and hope they continue to do the great things they set out to accomplish. Personally, I am the kind of guy who plans to comprehend every possible side of a problem in its entirety so I can then work on gathering every possible solution. Looking back, this approach ignited my desire to develop a program that can consider every single factor as time advances so that we can revolutionize the approach with all the most up-to-date information we know and one day get ahead of it. Up to this point, with what I now know, I see that we are so close to bringing an end to gun violence. Nonetheless, I knew I had to begin sharing what I know with many different people as I cannot do what I plan to do alone. This approach is where I need your help.

While researching prior school shootings, I wanted to understand why such tragedies were happening. When you look at these situations from the perpetrator's perspective--otherwise known as the shooter--it's pretty intriguing what you can find. The most common reason for gun violence in schools is due to an escalation of disputes (Riedman, 2023). This reasoning can include one or multiple situations like bullying, social exclusion, personal stressors, lack of intervention, or regular exposure to violent behaviors, which will build up pressure, shifting a person past their "breaking point" with the feeling that their best option is to proceed with harming others with a gun. This statistic in relativity to the variation of disputes is one of many factual elements that reconfigured my approach to finding research-backed solutions. Observing every piece of factual evidence while dissecting any other emerging components is imperative to do our best in comprehending the whole picture.

I wholeheartedly understand why some people have the belief that banning guns will solve the problem of gun violence in America. However, let's use substance abuse as an example. It does not matter what crime is associated with drug use and distribution. If someone is chasing a high from the use of a drug or even adding on the money they can make from distributing them, they will find a way to make it happen. The only difference with gun violence is the shooter is often looking to resolve their problem of feeling isolated from people, otherwise feeling alone in their struggles and believing that shooting other people will relieve them of that itch they've been attempting to scratch over a particular duration of time. Sadly for them, that is not the case. From what I've discovered thus far, it is my understanding that whether some people are struggling with substance abuse, or alcoholism, or social isolation, we first need to address the inner dialogue that is going on in their minds. By all means, I am not a medical or mental health professional, so there is a slight possibility I may be incorrect due to a misinterpretation of factual evidence from multiple credible sources. One thing I will not stop doing is working to find additional pieces of evidence that can either support my theory or even put up a solid argument to prove it wrong. I am sufficient with either case as long as it will lead us to the next probable solution to end the suffering of our students in school and any other person who is at risk of being harmed at any form of event or location.

One thing that blows my mind now that I am getting older—although I can relate to the feeling I had while in school—is the social status many students chase. There are always different groups of people with various labels, such as the "nerds," the "loners," and the "athletes," to name a few. I am proud to say that at one point in my life, I had all of these labels attached to my name and who knows what else people labeled me as. I was one of those kids who didn't care what people said about me, even though it hurt at times. However, one thing I never did was let people's words about me tear me down, as I believe that, as fellow humans, we shouldn't allow other people to decide how we feel. We may not have complete control over what they say about us yet, we can control how we move forward from that. My way of moving forward consisted of understanding why they may have said certain things about me—possibly because of something I said or did, or maybe something they are struggling with and they're trying to take it out on other people—and once I came to a consensus of what I may be able to do better starting right then and there, my process was complete, and I was ready to move on with my life. This approach may or may not be the best strategy for the situation. Yet, it is certainly better than what some other people have done. My approach differed when someone tried to bully my friends or others I loved. I can confidently say that if anyone has ever been "bullied" by me, they either messed with one of my friends or my family first. I can count the number of people I've been mean to in school on my fingers because I genuinely never wanted to cause any trouble. This method was simply an attempt to protect the people I love.

With that context from a more professional and personal level, this is the point where I have found a more structural level of thought pertaining to the social norms that our nation has placed on people in selective areas of our country. If we take my thoughts to an even deeper level, I don't care who society tells you you need to be. Thanks to the brave men and women in the military, you have the freedom to do whatever you want and become whoever you want to become. Parallel to that, my hope for each and every one of you, no matter where you're at in your life right now, is that you work to become the absolute best version of yourself that you can be. Another remarkable thing I discovered in numerous credible sources is that you can be happy by making other people happy with simple acts of kindness, as this is when your body produces what we like to call the "feel-good" chemicals. It's a goal of mine to work on practicing acts of kindness for people every day, and that's one of my challenges to you as well. One thing to remember in this process is to make sure you are acting kind to yourself. While on the topic of actions, I did mention earlier how my framework is established on a holistic, multi-factor approach of being proactive as opposed to reactive due to the many elements that lead to gun violence in addition to the various people in different industries and stages of life who are either directly or indirectly affected. In another portion of my ongoing research, where I am on the continuous hunt to discover ways that each person can be a part of the greater picture solution, this is some insight that I uncovered:

- For Students: They can take proactive steps, such as supporting peers, advocating for mental health resources, or starting conversations about safety amongst their student leaders;

- For Parents and/or Guardians: They can implement ways to foster open communication, recognize warning signs of distress, and advocate for better policies at schools;

- For Educators and Administrators: They can further develop practical strategies to make schools safer, from active shooter drills to enhanced security technology to fostering inclusive environments;

- For Mental Health and Healthcare Professionals: They can contribute by addressing trauma, supporting early intervention programs, and further their collaboration with schools;

- and For Law Enforcement: They can further strategize building trust with communities and prioritize de-escalation and prevention over reaction.

This short-form insight I shared here only touches the surface of what groups of people can make an impact and what each of these groups mentioned can do in their respective communities and professions. To bring more insight into advocacy, it comes down to all of us collectively speaking up for ourselves and others. It's not a simple task, though, as I struggle with speaking up for myself. Yet, I am practically always ready to go to bat for somebody else I care about. With advocacy, we must do this for ourselves and other people or causes that we support and believe in. By all means, never will I tell you that I am entirely correct just because I've researched specific topics. My opinion is always stated strictly based on the things I know at the time. I will invariably be willing to learn more, especially if plausible information proves me wrong, so my strategies may pivot, leading to a more practical solution. I will have to say, even though I may advocate in favor of or in opposition to specific policies within governmental environments from time to time, my research has led me to believe that most of what we can do in that setting is not very effective unless we take action in the other areas within our communities which again include mental health, anti-bullying, and the integration of technological advancements to safety and security systems in all locations. This course will be what helps us not only to get significantly ahead of any tragedy that may unfold but also to potentially prevent gun violence from even becoming a reality in the first place.

All that to say, you can do so much by taking various actions you believe in. I encourage you to do some of your own research for reference, and when you have something you want to change, step out, make it happen, and share it with the world. If the change is based on your own experiences, spread your message and see how you may positively impact others who may have experienced something similar, including things related to your health, your career, or any other part of your life that you hope to improve. Even if it is a particular type of policy that you want to support or oppose in your local, state, or federal government, reach out by email, letter, and phone to your respective elected officials and let them know how you feel to encourage them to vote the way you ask of them as your representative. Understand that, as an individual, you are strong. As you gather a team around you, you're not only adding to the change you are making, you are multiplying the impact!

CHAPTER TEN
BE THE CHANGE

"The measure of who we are is
what we do with what we have."
– Vince Lombardi

Every one of us humans has our own experiences from the moment we were brought onto this Earth that help shape who we are. The most extraordinary yet sometimes the most challenging part about life is no matter what the world throws at us, good or bad, we can decide how we react. If someone says something to you, will it go in one ear and out the other, or could it be something you hold onto? Indeed, depending on what they say and how you perceive it will determine the outcome. Now, if something happens to you, is it something you will forget about and go on with your life, or will it be something that sticks with you as a lasting memory forever? Similarly, depending on what happened to you and how you perceive that situation, it will likely conclude with a specific end result. Potentially, it is an outcome or effect that continues to recur over and over again unless one or more elements change, which may then pivot the direction negatively or positively, all dependent on what actions you take next. I say all of this to show you a glimpse of how strong you are at this very moment and how much stronger you can become if you believe in yourself.

When I decided to write this book, I knew I wanted to share a depiction of my story while diving into the direction I have chosen to go in my life. However, the one question that lingers in my head while writing is, "How do I hope this book will impact the amazing person who decides to read it?". As I continued thinking about that, I knew my hope for this book was to serve at least one of two purposes. The first mission and biggest hope is, as you finish reading this book, you feel inspired and empowered in a way that you know how amazing of a person you are and that you are ready to take the next steps in leveling up your life so that as each day goes by, you are becoming the happiest and healthiest version of yourself. If that is your only takeaway from this book, my heart will literally smile. Now, suppose I was able to achieve mission one. In that case, the second mission is that you were able to learn a little something extra related to this unfathomable world we live in and construct your own stance by taking action in the ways you feel are best in keeping everyone safe in schools, largely attended events, and highly populated areas. If you feel drawn to doing this, my heart might burst, but in a good way.

As I've mentioned, yes I have done the research. I currently have various strategies and resources that can be a great guide in the right direction. However, I will never stop seeking additional statistical data and human insight that can help reinforce or completely alter what my program currently offers. This philosophy is why a goal of mine is to speak to numerous different people, including you, to gain insight into your thoughts that could influence my approach or even make the greatest impact on someone else.

Hearing your thoughts and your story based on various experiences you have had throughout your lifetime so far would be a true honor. Please know that no matter your background or circumstances, you have the power to make a positive impact on anyone wherever you go. We were all born on this Earth for a purpose, and sadly, not many people discover their purpose while living this life. I hope that if you have found your purpose, you thrive in every possible way. If you haven't yet found your purpose, I aspire to be a stepping stone in your life to help you discover it and, to then again, thrive in every possible way. A challenge I have for you is to reflect on how far you have come in life up to this very moment. Who have you surrounded yourself with? What have you had to experience? When did you see something change in your life? Where do you feel you felt at your best and at your worst? Why were you in such an environment or situation? How could you have done something different to make it better and drive that change now?

All of these questions are relatively deep and may lead to some tough or, hopefully, exciting internal thoughts. Whatever the case may be, please know that you are loved, and amidst the people or places who may be against you, there is always someone rooting for you and wishing you the absolute best. I'm thankful to share this particular piece of encouragement with you because I can tell you, based on my experiences, even outside of being injured in a school shooting, have been nothing short of significantly deceptive. My goal is always to smile no matter what happens to me as I am genuinely grateful to be alive and live another day. Honestly, though, I do have days here and there where it is tough to get out of bed and do anything throughout those days. I often forget that I need to take care of myself before I can go out and help make a positive difference in the world. The other thing is knowing that I have made and continue to make plenty of mistakes in my life that I look back on and often beat myself up about, yet I have to remember that I am not perfect and never will be.

In the future, I'd love to share more about my other absurd life stories with you while hearing yours, too. However, the point I am trying to reinforce here is that we all have our own stories and beliefs that shape us into who we are and that the most incredible part of life is that we are here living it to tell our story, allowing us to impact others along the way. Alone, you can be the light to the nation. Together, we can bring light to the world. I share this with both you and myself alike when I say, have patience with yourself along the journey of discovering your purpose and taking action towards being the change, as it cannot happen overnight. Believe that you are capable of anything you set your mind to, and know that YOU ARE ENOUGH!

Keeping your purpose and the power of influence in mind, I invite you to consider joining me on this journey of ending gun violence in some way you may feel most empowered to conduct. I've mentioned that there is so much value in various perspectives, which is why I am always inclined to hear other people's stories. In alignment with this approach, multiple strategies have been shown to make a difference, yet have not been implemented simultaneously to make the overall impact of reversing the lines to decrease and one day end gun violence once and for all. Plus, I know for dang sure that I can't make this impact alone.

Some of these strategies are what I will share with you now. I plan to launch a podcast the same year this book is officially published, which has been a goal of mine for many years now where I can fully ignite another mission of mine to initiate the conversations on safety and mindful wellness, all rooted in lived experiences combined with personal and professional backgrounds, so that we can ultimately help to create better lives for everyone by keeping them happy, healthy, and safe. With this particular approach I plan to make with the podcast, we can uncover additional ways to keep people safe from gun violence and create stronger minds to overcome the rugged ways of this world while developing healthier bodies to feel the greatest they have ever felt. This approach all comes back to preventative measures that we can take to prevent gun violence proactively before it even starts, with the added benefit of positively impacting other lives in the process. For instance, together, we can also share insights with people that can influence them to create an even better life for themselves before allowing their lives and the lives around them to get into what I call the trench zone which can lead to significantly unhappy lives. Even if you may not be interested in sharing your story and perspectives on this podcast, I encourage you to start conversations in your community where you believe it can make a difference, letting your story be heard and fighting for the things in your heart.

Next up, support the various companies, organizations, and initiatives that share a mission that means a lot to you. It doesn't have to be on a monetary basis, either. It could be by sharing their posts on social media or telling a friend about them. Showing any support means a lot to those you share that collaborative mission with. I know I'm mentioning many of my missions for the program I have built over multiple years. However, if you decide to join in with the mission here or completely shy away from it, that's more than okay. The main thing I hope you take away from this portion is knowing that you have the voice to influence many, so please use it to make the world a better place. There are multiple companies, organizations, and initiatives relative to my own that also focus on mental wellness, school and event safety, prevention, and so much more that I also support. Remember, the larger a team you build around a particular cause, the greater multiplication you will see in the impact you make together.

The next strategy, which expands on sharing our stories, comes back to this book. In everything I do, I'm determined to make all of what I produce have meaning, such as the colors I use, specific text styles, various shapes, certain numbers, relative words, etc. This method includes how I do certain things, such as the preparation I do before speaking, the times I post or send out content, and even how I plan to release this book over a particular duration of time. Most everything I do has a specific meaning and purpose behind it, helping to make that much more of an impact on all who come across the things that I create. My ask to you is if you found any value in this book that has helped you in a remarkable kind of way, please share that with me through the review form at www.nathanielspeaks.com/yourthoughts as I'd love to see the impact this book had on you as the reader. Not to mention that your thoughts can also help me to become a better writer so that, hopefully, I may have the honor of you reading my future books where you may have an even better reading experience. In addition, if you feel this book can be a good read for anyone else, encourage them to get a copy, so together, we can multiply the impact of this book as well.

As for the next strategy, music is a massive way to share various messages, which is now something I hope to integrate into the impact I am attempting to make with all of you who join in on the missions of my program. It seems relevant to note here that never would I have thought I'd have the confidence nor expect myself to sing in front of other people, much less record myself singing and release it to the world to be steamed on all music platforms. Heck, I never even thought I could speak in front of a small group of people. However, I am proud to share that I've delivered a keynote to an audience of over 10,000. In fact, I've learned that being nervous before presenting to any size of crowd is crucial as it shows that you care about how your message will connect to the audience you are speaking to. Even to this day, I have the shakes and sweats before going in front of the room to speak to merely ten people. Yet, I now have the confidence to share a message I believe will make a difference in someone's life. When it comes to the impact of the message, I've seen how the messages I shared with students at schools, student leaders at conferences, believers in churches, and business executives within their companies have impacted them exceptionally well.

This area is where I have now made it a goal to strengthen my message while becoming a better presenter whenever I share a message with any audience of any size. While in the midst of becoming a better presenter and crafting a stronger message, this is where I felt that odd calling to integrate my own vocal music performances into the keynotes as it will multiply the impact I plan to make with the message. This technique circles back to my initial hope to make music and how it felt a part of my calling despite feeling completely uncomfortable doing so. This feeling goes all the way back to my first year of college when I felt the need to step out of my comfort zone and begin to learn how to sing. I took a course titled "Private Voice," where I met once a week with the vocal coach on campus to learn all about vocal techniques. Talk about being uncomfortable with singing. I had trouble gaining the confidence to simply do the vocal warm-ups we would practice at the beginning of each session, where I would match the pitch of the note played on the piano with a variation of I-E-A-O-U's, lip rolls, and R rolls. Then, I would sing portions of a favorite song of mine called "Reckless Love" by Cory Asbury. This part of the vocal lesson was the most difficult as my confidence was not there, and trying to sing a song by a vocal artist who is that great was stressful on a whole other level.

As we approached the end of the semester, we had already completed approximately 14 vocal lessons, and my vocal coach shared with me that there was a final exam I had to take to complete the course. At this point, I was ready to ace this final as I now had more confidence to sing this song in front of my vocal coach. However, she cut me off mid-sentence and shared that I would have to sing this song in front of about 75 people in the performance hall. My heart sank further and further after every word she spoke in that sentence. Seeing my shocked and terrified look, she said, "Nathaniel, the reason you have been so nervous about singing in front of people for this long is that you don't believe in the vocal talent you really do have." She followed with, "I've heard you sing these songs all semester and you sound amazing! The people who hear you sing in the performance hall will be blessed to hear your first vocal performance in front of a live audience, as the way you sing conveys a message that connects with those who hear it, and they will love every second of it. Now stop doubting yourself and do what you have done all semester." After hearing her say this, not only did it prepare me for the live performance, but it was also what rooted my idea to continue learning how to sing better over time and, one day, integrate a vocal performance, maybe even an original song of my own, into to messages I share with any audience to make that much more of an impact.

As the next few years went on, I hired a master vocal coach who trained many famous artists in today's music industry, including some of my favorite Christian music artists that I listen to today. This precise experience further set me on track to release my own music. Now, the real question I had for myself was what music style fits best with the message I wanted to share and my vocal type.

This moment is when I planned to release cover songs to kick off my music career for the first year of producing music for one of two reasons. The first was so that I could use amazing songs that I've listened to throughout my recovery time after the shooting and other parts of my life's growth journey overall. The second reason I wanted to release cover songs during the first year of producing music was to discover my singing voice further with various sub-genres of Christian-style music before I fully dive into the original music I want to create in the future.

As this strategy came to fruition, I realized I could go one step further and have another purpose for all I am creating by selecting songs to cover that signify each chapter I wrote in this book. Back in 2023, I began to look through all of my music playlists that I have listened to over the years and recall which songs helped me through various times of my life while, at the same time, symbolizing each chapter in this book. Then, the mission was on when it came to finding someone who could professionally record, mix, and master the songs that I had planned to cover and release out to the world.

Once that was all figured out, I was ready to craft my first cover song that would be the ultimate release to the world, which would also break the internal chain I had on myself for all these years to the fear of judgment and overall letting go of my tendency of always trying to make everything perfect before putting things out into the world. At this point, I am tired of allowing myself to be silent in some regions of my life, especially in the area of singing. I am ready to break free and not hold myself back within the confines of my comfort zone.

It is time that I actually become comfortable with being uncomfortable, as that is the only way we as humans will see growth over time. You will likely know this by the time you read this book as my first, and potentially a few other cover songs will be released on all streaming platforms. The coolest part is, as you are reading this book and perhaps even after you read the entire thing, there will be more cover songs released that connect back to each of the ten chapters in this book. You will see that context mentioned in assorted promotional content I release on social media and my website for the cover song releases.

The closing strategy that I ask you to consider joining in with me is helping to get my message heard by schools you are affiliated with, events you attend regularly, and even places many people, including you, go to often. Collectively, by joining in on any or even every strategy of this program that I've constructed, together, we will be one step closer to ending gun violence and, ultimately, preventing any person, any family, and any community from having to experience the horrific traumas of injury or death as a result of gun violence ever again. Not to mention that, as a result, together, we can help many people live a better life with improved health and a stronger mind.

In this chapter and the other nine chapters before this, there were so many stories throughout a large portion of my life and a multitude of information relative to the experiences and research I've done to create safer places for people to learn and have fun. Keeping that in mind, now seems like a good point to recap everything that went on in every chapter of this book, followed by the challenges I have for you from each chapter.

Looking back to the beginning of this story in Chapter One, I shared about the start of this stormy journey. Little did I know my life would be turned in an entirely new direction after this. The chapter not only brought insight into what my life was like before the tragedy yet, I hope it illustrated how no matter your age, background, social status, or any other kind of title this world attempts to label you as, your goals are accurate. You should do everything you can to achieve them, no matter who or what tries to stop you. My goals when it came to being more social with friends, more athletic with sports, and more experienced with breaking out of my comfort zone were definitely met, if not exceeded. That brings me to challenge you to step out of your comfort zone and do whatever it takes to achieve your goals from this point forward. While on this growth journey of your own, be intentional with breaking the goals down into the smallest and most simple steps possible and spread it out by the week, by the day, or even by the hour to bring the goal into a perception that looks much more achievable.

In Chapter Two, you indirectly witnessed what the day of January 14th, 2014, looked like from my perspective.

The crisis presented here reinforces the proven statement that not every day is promised. To be completely honest, with all of what my family has experienced over the years, we know that statement all too well. I am thankful that most of us are still here and live to tell a story. Relative to the fact that every day is not promised, my challenge to you is to live every day as if it's your last and live it in a way where you take logical chances that have the potential to change your life and the lives of those around you for the better. In other words—and I'm also challenging myself while writing this—learn when to say yes and when to say no. The time we have in this life is limited, and I hope that none of us get toward the end of our lives, regretting a large part of how we lived it.

In Chapter Three, you took a peek into the world inside my head where I told of the dreams I was having while sedated in the hospital. This was followed by my transition back into the real world, where I entered the very beginning of a long road to recovery in the hospital and a physical rehabilitation center after that. There were a few wins in this chapter, considering that my life was not over yet, including the act of forgiveness being possible, the ways I was able to overcome the many things medicine claimed I wouldn't be able to do, and the reconnection with my hometown with a welcome home parade that I will cherish forever. The context throughout this part of my life signifies that no matter what happens to you—mentally, physically, spiritually, emotionally, or the alike—you have the power to determine how you move forward from that point onward. With the spiritual faith that I have, knowing that forgiveness is ever present, I knew that if I forgave the shooter right then and there, it would set me on a path toward accelerated healing all around. This methodology does not mean that I approve of what he did. It only reiterates the point that I know I am not perfect, yet I am still forgiven. If I seek forgiveness for my wrongdoings, I, too, shall forgive those who do wrong to me. In alignment with that, I challenge you to reflect on all the harsh and potentially horrific things that have happened in your life and even the wrong people have done to you. After reflecting, ask yourself, "Am I allowing anything or anyone from my past to hold me back?". If you answer yes, ask yourself, "How can I forgive them or forgive myself in order to move past this and become better because of it?". Again, just because you are forgiving someone or even yourself for any wrongdoings of the past does not mean you approve of what happened. You are only allowing yourself to break the chains to those hurts and move on, living free from what has been holding you down for a long time. In alignment with my Christian faith, I often like to say, "Let go and Let God!". However, if this does not align with your personal beliefs, I respect that. Just know that however you decide to approach this situation, you must forgive in order to break free from the things that are holding you back.

Chapter Four took a deep dive into the Summer Break

following the shooting. You took a look into some more cool experiences I was blessed with, more insane surgical procedures on the journey to improving my vision as much as possible, the major adjustments I had to make to my learning environment in school now that I am considered legally blind, and even a step into the courtroom with me when it was time to sentence the shooter who nearly ending my life and left hundreds if not thousands of other lives forever changed because of his actions. As you have seen, there were many challenging and difficult times at this point in my life. Yet, my perspective through it all was knowing that I survived this incident for a reason. I had an entirely new purpose for my life, which meant there was no time to sit there and complain or be angry with anyone or angry about anything. My challenge for you here is to accept the things in life that you cannot control and take charge of the things you can control. For instance, you can't control what people think of you. However, you can control what you do in your life and how you act, influencing what the people you care most about think of you. Understand that you will never please everyone, so make it a point to please those who believe in the mission you intend to live out.

Chapter Five was about when I returned to school, the very school where my life was nearly over, to finish the remainder of my middle school education. This span was also slightly difficult as I was still adjusting to new learning styles with assistive technology that I often hesitated to use. My social circle shrunk due to my eye not seeing very well and some false perceptions that I purposely didn't talk to certain people anymore, even though I couldn't tell who they were if they were standing right in front of me. There were many good times in the mix of it all, though, especially when I was able to be my brother's best man at his wedding. Speaking of good parts, the additional people aside from my amazing family who came into my life and helped me to power through the transition to this new life of mine, specifically within my education, was a complete blessing. I stand firm when I say that if it wasn't for these few influential men and women I had supporting me throughout middle school and high school, as highlighted further in Chapter Six, I wouldn't have been able to finish out the remainder of my K-12 education as successfully as I did.

During this time, there were many friends that I was no longer connected to, which hurt me. Yet, very excellent people came into my life at this time, which helped my life become better because of it. I'm sure you've heard the saying, "You are the people you spend the most time with," or at least some variation of it. This saying reigned true for me at this time in my life, and it was a big lesson to me as to who I should be spending more time with and who I may need to shift away from a little more. With this concept in mind, my challenge for you is to access the people with whom you spend the most time. Are they helping or supporting you toward your growth of becoming your best self, or are they holding you back? On the contrary, are you helping them to grow, or are you holding them back? Specifically, with those you discover are the people holding you back, in the most respectful way--more out of respect for yourself--make it a point to limit how much time you spend with them or even completely stop spending time with those people. It may hurt at that very moment, but your life is projected to become better because of it. Don't forget to also find other people who do extraordinary things you want to do and support your ambitions so that, again, you can become the people you spend the most time with.

Chapter Six highlights the wild passage I had throughout high school, ranging from my exploration of student organizations, jumping into one of my first jobs, and taking advantage of the many leadership development opportunities I had right at my fingertips. I was thankful to still have the support from my family and a few specific, very special people who helped me stay on track with my education while pursuing all of my other rambunctious ambitions. At this time in my life, I was determined to pursue medical school after high school and become a Pediatric Trauma Surgeon, as that's where I felt called in that era. I have to say this was also a point in my life where I allowed my sleep schedule to become very misaligned. Despite my age, the exhaustion was already catching up to me in many ways. I say that because it has come to my awareness that many people, maybe even you, struggle with this same thing of prioritizing rest. That said, as a challenge for both you and me, let's make it a priority to get to sleep and wake up at the same time every day, including weekends while getting anywhere from 7-9 hours of quality sleep each night. By all means, I am no somnologist—otherwise known as a sleep doctor—although, with the credible evidence I've discovered over the years of doing personal research on sleep, that's what I've seen as a common directive by a large majority if not all professionals in this field. All that to say, let's get good sleep for a change so, in return, we can live a better life, pursuing all of the unique ambitions we have for ourselves.

Chapter Seven laid out the roller coaster of emotions with many successes and failures as I was now more in a mentor-style role within organizations I was previously a member of while still pursuing advancement alongside them in addition to my attempt at managing the new college life where I felt rather lost in the beginning. Thankfully, I had some outstanding achievements that helped me overcome the hurts of the failures I was experiencing then. Yet, I learned something bigger in these moments, and that is the fact that failure isn't fatal. In addition, if you use all of your failures as fuel to learn what to do and what not to do next time, you are using it as power toward success. Now, I challenge you to utilize this concept with any failures you have experienced in the past or may be going through right now and help yourself to discover a learning opportunity from each of them so that you can become better the next time you come across that same kind of challenge or situation. In other words, take your losses, learn from them, and from that point, you will win.

Speaking of wins, as we went into Chapter Eight, I began to see the light at the end of the tunnel, and it seemed my life finally had a great sense of clear direction. I transferred to another university and changed my major, which felt slightly right. It still took me a minute to declare my final major in Business Administration. Yet, I was able to engage with additional opportunities within the entrepreneurship realm, which ultimately led me to discover the area where I truly felt called and most everything felt right. Not to mention the fact that I was also contracted with an exceptional company at this time, and it helped me to further my experience in public speaking through leadership development on top of guiding me toward the greater part of my personal mission for the company of my own I started not long before being contracted with them where I aimed to speak in various places to make an impact of creating safer places while overall, creating better lives. Change is a good thing. With that in mind, my challenge to you is to embrace change. It may be challenging at first, as it was a challenge for me to change my educational path in an entirely new direction. However, I know I am better because of that change. Whether it be a job, your education, or anything else that may currently be bringing you down in your personal or professional life, dissect every detail and see what needs to be changed. Now, don't go changing every single thing right off the bat. Take it one step at a time and see what works best for you. In what ways are you becoming more happy and healthy? There will continue to be bumps in the road, but the question is, "Are you happy with what is on the other side of the mountain to the point where it is worth climbing?" Face the changes that need to be made and live it. Embrace it!

As mentioned before, change is a good thing. In Chapter Nine, you see the mission that I have set out in full force to spread the school and event safety program I initially started working on ever since my Senior project in high school, even though I didn't know it at the time. Yet, this mission is becoming so much bigger as it is now a part of my career where I hope to make an impact with intense multiplication to save the masses and make life better for everyone. This stretch is where it became more apparent that I could not do what needed to be done alone. Yet, I uncovered a large majority of the solutions that can make a difference as credible sources from my research back the strategy. It also became clear that research is not enough, which is why I set out to strategize additional ways to gather more information from the real world instead of research articles. There is so much more we can continue to learn collectively about ourselves and the lives and elements of life around us. I now challenge you to do some activities or research in various ways for yourself to discover more about who you really are, who other people are—especially those people who you look up to—and about things you care about to grasp the knowledge and learn what you can do to make a difference.

As we reached the final stretch of Chapter Ten, most everything began to come together as we looked into the basics of becoming the happiest and healthiest versions of ourselves. Once we are in a state of change, we can make things better in our own lives as we now have the power to go out and help people worldwide get one step closer to the happiest and healthiest versions of themselves. I clearly understand that it was somewhat slippery when it came time for me to experience change by diving into the unknown. However, I knew that discovering what was on the other side by taking an uncharted zone and learning as I went was so worth the fact that I just lived it out and enjoyed the ride at every step. I invite you to take on the challenge of writing down ten goals that you have. After writing them out, make an action list with three points for each goal, which consists of the three actions you can take to advance toward each of those ten goals. A guiding principle that we must consider along this journey of action is to learn from every failure and celebrate all the wins, as this will be what brings your vision to life.

Phew! That's quite a hefty amount of insight into the life of Nathaniel over the course of ten chapters. Although there is so much more to cover when it comes to how, in the world, we are called to action to guide people towards greater lives from the youngest of ages so, in turn, we can get significantly ahead of this currently rising gun violence catastrophe while pursuing additional holistic routes which include multiple factors which could very well serve a more substantial part in the overall solution to this problem.

Considering the depth of my research along with various engagements I've had with the public, there are many works that I plan on producing in the very near future, especially as I continue to build upon these findings with your help through future books, research articles, keynote performances, music productions, and who knows what else. A collective goal for all of us is to do whatever it takes to find peace in this world, starting by ending the horrific tragedies we are currently seeing as a result of countless perpetrators discharging firearms all across America in schools, churches, shopping centers, and largely attended events like concerts to name a few. With your help, I aim to continue working alongside other transformational people like you and organizations who are doing what they can to help find a long-term solution to this problem in order to integrate the proactive, multi-factor approach rather than the "one thing will change it all," reactive mindset. Imagine how much greater life will be for you, your students, and your families, knowing that nobody has to worry any longer about getting injured or dying because of a shooter.

If you're a teacher, think about how you won't have to worry about your students or yourself when it comes to your safety from gun violence. Envision how those of you who attend church services won't have to worry about the enemy coming in to steal, kill, and destroy the lives within the sanctuary. Visualize yourself and your friends and family being able to go places like the movies, shopping centers, concerts, or anything else fun without having to worry about the safety of yourself and those you love being at risk, all because of the person being the weapon.

As I've mentioned before, I am not perfect. Nobody is perfect. It's not like we live in an ideal world. Sadly, the world itself will never be perfect. At least not in this lifetime. The point is, what can we do, and how can we do everything in our power to ensure we can all live the best life possible during our time on this Earth? I'm sure by now, you and I share a very common, if not exact, vision for the future pertaining to safety from shooting catastrophes. I ask that you join me in these efforts, as there is no way that I or the other actively working individuals on this issue can do it alone. Whether it's reaching out to me by any means of communication, encouraging others to purchase this book, starting conversations on this topic in your community, having me speak to a certain audience you are a part of, or any other action in alignment with my program or this overall mission, you are helping to be the change through discovery and execution.

Remember, you have the power to do so many great things in this world that will allow you to make a huge difference by simply expanding on your acts of kindness, which spread hope. With your efforts, we will be able to continue multiplying the impact of this mission. I thank you from the bottom of my heart, not only for investing in this book but also for your willingness to support the bigger picture being constructed here. Not only do I hope you were able to gain greater understanding through this story, yet also have a feeling that you may too be called to action. There is a concept called the ripple effect, where one person's actions can inspire others, creating a ripple of positive change, which aligns with my goal here. Across this journey of tragedy, tribulation, and triumph that we took together in this book, we can accurately project that other lives will continue to see a similar pattern. However, no matter the tragedy, we will be able to power through it; no matter the tribulations, we will be able to overcome them; and no matter the triumphs, we will be able to continue winning as together, we can make the world a better place. Always believe in what you have the power to do, build a team around the mission you feel is right, and live out that purpose with every ounce you have within you. Together, let's BE THE CHANGE!

What impact did the book ////////// have on you? //////////

 Leave Your Review Here

www.nathanielspeaks.com/yourthoughts

Connect with
NATHANIEL

f 	 in 	
@nathanielrtavarez

READY TO MAKE AN IMPACT TOGETHER?

Connect with Nathaniel to speak at your:

- School
- Conference
- Church
- Business
- Policy Session
- or Any Event!

 www.nathanielspeaks.com

Listen to the lastest music by
NATHANIEL TAVAREZ

Streaming on All Music Platforms

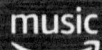 Spotify YouTube MUSIC